LBJ'S MORTAL WOUND

The Don Reynolds Story
— THE PRESIDENT — THE BOBBY BAKER SCANDAL — DALLAS —

A FAMILY MEMOIR BY
BOB NELSON

LBJ'S MORTAL WOUND: THE DON REYNOLDS STORY
Copyright © 2023/2024 Bob Nelson. All Rights Reserved.

Published by:
Trine Day LLC
PO Box 577
Walterville, OR 97489
1-800-556-2012
www.TrineDay.com
trineday@icloud.com

Library of Congress Control Number: 2024944722

Nelson, Bob,
LBJ's Mortal Wound—1st ed.
p. cm.

Epub (ISBN-13) 978-1-63424-465-7
Trade Paper (ISBN-13) 978-1-63424-464-0

1. Donald Buck Reynolds (1915-1993) 2. JFK assassination 3. Political corruption United States 4. United States Politics and government 1945- . 5. Family. I. Nelson, Bob. II. Title

[Note: Throughout the book, I have chosen to capitalize the word "President" out of my personal respect for the importance of the office of the leader of our country. I realize that some may not agree with this, but it is my particular preference. – Bob Nelson.]

First Edition
10 9 8 7 6 5 4 3 2 1

Distribution to the Trade by:
Independent Publishers Group (IPG)
814 North Franklin Street
Chicago, Illinois 60610
312.337.0747
www.ipgbook.com

> "How come I haven't heard about this?"
> –Jim Dedelow, Announcer
> WJOB Radio,
> Hammond, Indiana
> October 11, 2023

> "Don, we are Masons. I just want to tip you off. Leave the country, leave the States. If you don't, LBJ will have you killed."
> –J. Edgar Hoover, head of FBI to Don Reynolds;
> as recounted by Don Reynolds to a family friend in 1969

Contents

Acknowledgments x
Prologue by Phil Singer 1
Preface 5
Introduction 13
1) What Started It All – November 22, 1963 15
2) The End of Family Secrets – April 2019 19
3) LBJ's Crisis In Copenhagen – October 1963 21
4) Family History, Assassination, and A Star Witness 23
5) A Family In The Spotlight & Private Presidential Panic – December 1963-March 1964 .. 31
6) Correspondence & A Senate Conclusion 39
7) Judging, Trust, and Two Senate Witnesses – March 1964 43
8) A Mysterious Fire, The Senate Shocker, LBJ's Fourth Crisis, and A Secreted Star 51
9) Senate Testimony & A Senate Sham – December 1964-March 1965 61
10) The Aftermath 71
11) The Years Of Exile And The Times Of Trouble –1964-1968 77
12) 25 Years Of Family Secrets – 1968-1993 95
13) Don Reynolds – Crude Or Compassionate? 101
14) Family Life, A Return to the Senate, And Exploring the Past – 1993-2022 107
15) What If? 115
16) Triumph, Tragedy, and Tyranny 117
Postscript by Gregory T. Smith 121
Epilogue 123
Index 133
Addendum I) A Tale of Three Cities by Phil Singer 151
Addendum II) Getting Closer To The Truth by Phil Singer 155
Addendum III) What's New? What's Old? by Phil Singer 159

Donald Buck Renyolds – circa 1945

This book is dedicated to my Uncle Buck – Don Reynolds – for his courage and inspiration.

Unsolved Mysteries in this Unfolding Drama

1. 11/22/63:
   Drama: Three cities at the same time. Three for the price of one: Dallas, Washington and New York.
   Mystery: Why has the media been silent or nonobservant? It has not been fully told. Dallas, not Washington, not New York.

2. Pulitzer Prize winners writing:
   Drama: Testimony During Disaster, a chapter in Mollenhoff's *Despoilers of Democracy*, 1965. Robert Caro: "unbelievably dramatic" "no writes about this."
   Mystery: Caro did not mention Mollenhoff. He wrote about this in 1965. Why did Caro omit Mollenhoff's work?

3. LBJ's Secret White House Tapes:
   Drama: "I'm going to jail!" "You have to defend me." Moyers was in the room.
   Mystery: Why has Moyers been silent for all these years? I reached out to his publicist; who said Moyers "had no time."

4. Family Drama:
   Drama: LBJ vs. The Kennedys. Chasing Demons on Vimeo, History Channel.
   Mystery: Reynolds left the country. Was Don Reynolds ever contacted?

5. FBI:
   Drama: FBI 17,571 pages, 3 1/2 years.
   Mystery: No response. Why?

6. Farmhouse Fire:
   Drama: Don Reynolds' farmhouse strangely burned down in 1964
   Mystery: Unsolved.

* * *

If anyone has information on these mysteries, please contact the author and/or the publisher.

Film Credits

Available On You Tube

LBJ:

1. *From Senate Majority Leader* (Robert Caro) 12:00--15:05.

2. *Accidental Presidents* – (Jared Cohen, C-Span) 58:00-60:00.

3. *The Open Mind* – Part 3 of 3 – *The Passage of Power* (Robert Caro) 2:45-8:00.

4. *The Men Who Killed Kennedy* (History Channel, Part 9) 14:00-15:20.

5. *The Man Who Killed Kennedy* (Book TV, Roger Stone) 4:50-6:00.

6. *LBJ vs. Kennedy* (Chasing Demons On Vimeo, History Channel) 12:45-19:00. (Currently unavailable due to copyright dispute.)

7. *America's Untold Stories* – *Did LBJ Kill JFK* (Mark Groubert) 15:00--17:30; 39:10--41:30.

LBJ Legacy and Don B. Reynolds

1. "I had a cabinet full of documents, Bill. We could have taken down the president."
    - Senator John Williams (DE) to Senator Bill Roth (DE), *The John Williams Papers*

2. "I don't want history to say these things. I don't want to be a Harding."
    - *LBJ worried about Don Reynolds' revelations. LBJ secret tapes. Johnson was referencing former President Warren G. Harding, 1921-23. After his death, a number os scandals were exposed which damaged his reputation.*

3. "I don't want to go against your judgment, because you've got to defend me. But if I do, I'm going to jail."

    - *LBJ to Atty Abe Fortas, who counseled LBJ to tell his story re: Don Reynolds. But LBJ feared if he told his story re:Reynolds, he would go to jail. LBJ secret tapes*

CONCLUSION: Where the Watergate and Lewinski scandals produced resignation or impeachment, Johnson got away with obstructing legislative and administrative inquiries."

    - *All The Way With LBJ*, Robert Wood Johnson

CONCLUSION:

"Reynolds' testimony tarnished Johnson's reputation and legacy."

"Reynolds' testimony remains a crucial piece of the puzzle when examining the Johnson administration..."

"In summary, the Don B. Reynolds testimony had a *lasting impact on American history*, particularly in relation to Lyndon B. Johnson … his role in exposing corruption *remains significant*."

    - *Microsoft Bing*

Acknowledgments

I would like to thank Lee Grady at the Wisconsin Historical Society, Rebecca Johnson at the University of Delaware, and Mary Joe Miller and Matt Piersoll at the University of Nebraska for their thorough assistance in accessing my uncle's archives.

I would also like to thank two friends of the family (who wish to remain nameless), who were invaluable in locating family papers and for giving perspectives on my uncle, Don Reynolds.

For early release of the LBJ tapes, my thanks go to Lady Byrd Johnson and Harry Middleton of the LBJ Library.

The University of Wisconsin Pathway to Publication program kept me disciplined and on the right track. I give big thanks to Laurie Scheer, a member of the program, for her excellent guidance.

Thanks go to researcher Greg Smith, from History Piquette, who helped guide me through the FOIA process with the FBI, CIA, and Pentagon files of my uncle. Thanks to Brandon Bernicky, who was great with web page development.

TrineDay Publications head, Kris Millegan, gave me the chance to write. Many thanks to you and to assistant, Michelle Fulton. Phil Singer from suburban Chicago was meticulous in guiding the project from beginning to end.

I thank my wife and daughter for enduring the long days and months of writing and research and their patient understanding.

Lastly, my heartfelt gratitude goes out to the late Senator Curtis, and particularly Senator John Williams, who kept the inquiry alive and in the history books. God bless you, Senator Williams. How we need you now!

Prologue

Don "Uncle Buck" Reynolds Thrown Into History

Some people consciously try to become famous. Or break a record. Many people want to go down in history for some type of achievement. Think of Olympic athletes. Or professional baseball players, for example. Sometimes it's just some weird obscure thing that'll get you or a group of friends or co-workers in the "Guinness Book of World Records." And there's nothing wrong with trying to achieve, or accomplish, these things. But many times, people are just thrown into history. They become famous, although that was not their intention at all.

I am a long-time John F. Kennedy assassination researcher. And I have met, and have become friends with, quite a few important people involved in some aspect of the case. An example: to this day, I stay in touch with Mary Ann Moorman, who is 92. Mary and her girlfriend Jean Hill were excited to see President Kennedy when he came to Dallas on November 22nd, 1963. They were also very much looking forward to seeing Jackie, the President's wife. And wanted to see what she was wearing. Jackie was almost like a rock star to many people. She was quite pretty and very stylish. Mary's son Ricky had asked if he could go to the parade that day to see the President. Mary told him that he needed to stay in school, but that she would take a picture for him. Mary had a Polaroid camera. As it turned out, Mary and Jean took a position in Dealey Plaza, just a few feet south of Elm Street on the grass. They had been there for a little while. And then the motorcade arrived. It made a right turn from Main Street onto Houston, followed by a sharp left turn onto Elm.

Suddenly, the limousine with President Kennedy was moving west on Elm Street towards Mary and Jean. And then there were some loud noises. Many people that were there thought that they were hearing firecrackers going off – at least, at first. Just as the limo, from right to left, passed the two women, Mary took a photograph. It was black and white. Mary and Jean were close enough to hear Jackie cry out that her husband had been shot. Then Mary and Jean got down, realizing that the sounds that they were hearing were bullets being fired. This particular picture shows Jackie and her husband, President Kennedy, with the famous grassy knoll and the picket fence in the background. It is considered an iconic photograph, taken during the shooting sequence on Elm Street. This photo has been studied by researchers for decades.

Well, Mary and Jean Hill were just spectators that day in Dallas. But boy, they sure got thrown into history! There are interviews of them from that day that you can find on the Internet. Go to YouTube and you'll find a lot of things about these women. I knew Jean too and she also unintentionally became famous as an important Kennedy witness. They were just two of many that got thrown into history that day. There were other witnesses to the shooting, of course. And there were policemen and deputy sheriffs and doctors and nurses and Secret Service agents and people at the autopsy of the President, etc. These things happen to ordinary people.

Well, this is what the book that you're holding is about. The Don Reynolds story, written by his nephew Bob Nelson, is about how Uncle Buck also got thrown into history. Don was an insurance salesman and got caught up in dealings with Senator and then-Vice President Lyndon Baines Johnson. Johnson, who had experienced a heart attack in the 1950s, needed some life insurance. Don Reynolds was able to help out Johnson. But Johnson wanted some kickbacks, which Reynolds described more like a "shakedown." This all led to Reynolds giving sworn testimony on November 22nd, 1963, in Washington, D.C. - just as Kennedy was shot to death in front of his own wife in Dallas. This book will fill you in on what transpired, concerning President Johnson, the F.B.I. and threats – forcing Reynolds to flee the country. And how it all affected a young Bob Nelson, the book's author.

I have been working with author Bob Nelson for a couple of years now, meeting with him to assist him in this book project. On many occasions, we would meet at Las Palmas restaurant in Westmont, Illinois with computer and Internet expert Brandon Bernicky and his lovely wife Liezl. We discussed many things and accomplished a lot. We got Bob a website [www.thedonreynoldsstory.com] and some speaking engagements. Brandon and I got Bob some very cool two-sided business cards made with a lot of information about his Uncle Buck [Don Reynolds]. Brandon was able to digitize an audio cassette that Bob had of his uncle from the 1960s. It's quite revealing in a cryptic kind of way. And can be found on Bob's website, mentioned up above. When President Kennedy was killed, Bob was just ten years old, living in Munster, Indiana. Also, meeting with Bob at the restaurant, was

J.F.K. researcher Jim Gochenaur from Milwaukee and Antoinette Giancana [Chicago mobster Sam's daughter] from time to time. [Sadly, Jim died earlier this year.] These lunch-time meetings allowed all of us to discuss many aspects of Bob's story about his uncle Don Reynolds, and everyone was able to make suggestions about the book and its contents. We also met with Abraham Bolden at his house in Chicago. Abraham was the first African American Secret Service agent on the White House detail. He was hand-picked by President Kennedy in 1961. When Abraham tried to come forward to the Warren Commission in early '64 with some information about some things that he had observed, he landed in prison. But Abraham had the courage to document his story in a book *The Echo from Dealey Plaza* in 2008.

We discovered early on, the passion in Bob about getting this story out to the public. When I mentioned to him about how his uncle got "thrown into history," Bob really liked that phrase. Because it was so true. I was able to help get Bob a publisher for his book – someone that I have known for many years: Kris Millegan of TrineDay in Oregon. Kris and TrineDay have the courage to publish many books that other book publishers don't want to touch due to their sensitive and controversial nature.

Don Reynolds is mentioned in quite a few books about Johnson and/or Kennedy. A couple of examples of this are: 1964's *A Texan Looks at Lyndon* by J. Evetts Haley. This book came out in March of '64, well before the Warren Report was even published. In 1968, there's a whole chapter about Don Reynolds in *The Dark Side of Lyndon Baines Johnson* by Joachim Joesten. Chapter 24 is titled "Sing No More, Don Reynolds!"

So – the Reynolds story isn't new. It's just not very well known. This book, that you're presently holding, will hopefully change that. Author Bob Nelson is filling us in on his mother's brother and the often-ugly underside of Washington, D.C. politics. It's about how almost anyone can get caught up in things, for whatever reasons, that you'll likely regret later. You can get in way over your head, so to speak.

By the way, Bob Nelson can be reached by e-mail at: rrhfnel@aol.com. This e-mail address is on his already-mentioned two-sided business card that we made for the book.

Don Reynolds – a.k.a. Uncle Buck – got thrown into history alright. And so did his nephew Bob, the book's author. Enjoy the reading, as you discover their true and amazing story.

-Phil Singer, Illinois, September 2024.

My Uncle Buck and my grandfather in Lamar, South Carolina, Circa 1956

Preface

And I saw one of his heads as it were wounded to death; and his deadly wound was healed: and all the world wondered after the beast.
– Revelation 13:3

"You've got quite a family, haven't you?"

I was in the capital of Wisconsin at the east side FedEx print shop. The service person in charge had noticed some of my chapter titles: Assassination and a Star Witness, Senate Testimony and a Senate Sham, 25 Years of Family Secrets...

Her comment got me thinking more about my family: the Reynolds-Nelson clan. The extraordinary events of my uncle's life had impacted us all. What other family so poignantly felt the shock waves that radiated from the quake that Don Buck Reynolds, my "Uncle Buck," had initiated? He had given evidence against the sitting Vice President of the United States and was mentioned on the secret LBJ presidential tapes – prompting LBJ to say, "I don't want to be a Harding!" and, "I'm going to jail!" He fled the United States for fear of retaliation by the President, racked up a backlog of potential felonies, was the focus of over 17,000 pages of FBI documents, suffered an IRS judgment worth over $1,000,000 today, was constantly surveilled by the FBI, received death threats, was featured on numerous programs like the History Channel, was written about by two Pulitzer Prize winners, and gave testimony that could have taken a sitting president down! (Author Phillip Nelson said that my Uncle Buck's impending testimony spurred LBJ to commit the "crime of the century.") At that time, the foundation seemed to shake endlessly as Uncle Buck's family, my family, desperately tried to seek out stability.

***

Don B. Reynolds, through the transformational national event of JFK's assassination, is the only person in U.S. history to be a vice presidential, and presidential, whistleblower, and I had a front-row seat as the drama unfolded! Few of the players have ever spoken about their experiences; Bobby

Baker's kids, and Luci and Lynda Byrd Johnson, have said nothing. Bobby Baker and Bill Moyers refused to talk with Pulitzer Prize winner, Robert Caro – who has written four volumes on LBJ. (I, myself, reached out to Moyers; I received a polite reply from his publicist that Moyers "had no time.")

I found it odd that Baker was the only one who had written about it. Was there a reason why no one else wanted to drill down and uncover potential secrets hitherto undiscovered? I knew it was going to be up to me to share what I knew about my family's story. I didn't want to rely solely on my own experiences and memories; I was prepared to dive deeply.

***

Back in 2019, I went to the University of Wisconsin to see Pulitzer Prize winner, David Maraniss, give a talk about his book, *A Good American Family: The Red Scare and My Father*. It seemed as if his father, and my uncle, had both faced challenges in the U.S. Senate, although at different times and under different circumstances.

Maraniss signed his book to me, "Bob, good luck on your book project." He then asked me a question, "Have you heard of Bob Caro?"

I nodded.

He told me to take the famous author's advice to "turn every page."

Serendipitously, just 100 yards from where I spoke with Maraniss, was a treasure trove of pages about my Uncle Buck, collected by Clark Mollenhoff, on the Baker scandal. Mollenhoff had gone to Drake University, but his collection on the Bobby Baker scandal wound up at the Wisconsin Historical Society!

In January 2020, I was at the University of Delaware at Newark researching the Senator John J. Williams papers about Bobby Baker and my Uncle Buck.

"Did you read *Wheeling and Dealing* by Bobby Baker?" asked Rebecca Johnson, President Biden's Senate archivist.

My answer was a flat "Yes," but her question was important.

She knew about Delaware Senator John Williams, the "Conscience of the U.S. Senate," and she knew about his battles with LBJ, Bobby Baker, and the senator's unflagging support of my uncle. She also told me that Ina Caro, the wife of Robert Caro, had come to the archives to do research on John Williams for her husband's fourth book on LBJ, *The Passage of Power*.

Rebecca pointed me in the direction I needed to go, and the archives did not disappoint. Senator Williams had a habit of collecting everything, either in the Congressional Record, or from private correspondence. My uncle's communications to him, as well as his own letters, were a rich find. There was even a recording of the 1964 broadcast of *Face the Nation,* where Senator Williams mentioned my uncle in conjunction with the scandal.

Buoyed by my experience in the archives, and despite COVID-19 dangers, I journeyed back to the East Coast in the summer of 2020. I stopped at my uncle's childhood home to receive some family documents – and a warning. "If you keep digging, don't be surprised if you find something you won't like," admonished a friend of the family. His advice turned out to be prescient. In an inside family joke, referring to my uncle's fleeing to the Bahamas, he then asked me if I had my plane ticket to Nassau ready.

I then briefly visited Bobby Baker's hometown of Easely, South Carolina. I traveled to Ocean City, Maryland, where Bobby Baker built The Carousel, the motel for the advise-and-consent crowd, or, as one person called it, "a summer congressional cathouse."

I swam in the warm ocean waters directly in front of The Carousel, trying to think about what it must have been like in the early 1960s, in the heyday before Baker's fall. I was in the general area where Baker's lover and secretary, Carole Tyler, died in a plane crash in 1965, after taking off from the Ocean City airport.

Oakland, Maryland was the last stop. I had spent many summers there with my Uncle Buck and Aunt Jerry (Geraldine Wilkerson, my uncle's second wife) as a young boy. At the city library archives, I was able to locate newspaper articles from the *Oakland Gazette* on Uncle Buck and Bobby Baker. (A key article was from August 1964 on my uncle's farmhouse fire.)

I drove to Deep Creek Lake where I had spent idyllic summers swimming and boating with my uncle. The vintage, red brick façade of Englanders Grill and Soda Fountain was still there; the Maryland icon was just as inviting as it ever was. I also went to the site of my uncle's farm. I met Dan Beckman – my uncle's neighbor who knew about his farmhouse fire – and Stuart Thayer, who told me about the movie stars who had visited my uncle's farmhouse … and how my uncle had hid on rural farms after the scandal broke.

In September, I traveled to the University of Nebraska at Lincoln and was able to collect Senator Carl Curtis' archives on the Bobby Baker scandal and my uncle. Senator Curtis had passed the bar exam without law school. After reading some of his papers, I could see why. He was instrumental in day-to-day legal battles to uncover the truth.

7

On January 29, 2021, I received a call from my archivist and researcher, Greg Smith. He noted that we had made some progress getting FBI information. We talked about the big agencies: the CIA, FBI, IRS, and the Pentagon. I casually mentioned that a friend of the family said a resident of my uncle's hometown had worked for the CIA and had met my uncle in Mexico City, during his years of exile. When this person got back to CIA headquarters in Langley, his boss asked, "Why were you talking to Don Reynolds?"

Greg said, "Really. It wouldn't surprise me if they're listening to us now…"

As of 2021, the list of mysteries to unravel was daunting, particularly for someone who was already working two jobs (sixty to seventy hours a week). I couldn't get past feeling that a lot of progress had been made, but that there were still too many missing pieces. For a personality type that wanted to get every bit of information, it was a tough situation to accept.

What was the relationship between LBJ and my aunt and uncle's huge tax judgments? (On tape, LBJ had said to Sheldon Cohen, IRS Commissioner, "Get tough on Reynolds") Did my aunt and uncle divorce because of the huge tax judgment, or some other reason? The farmhouse fire in Oakland, Maryland was very suspicious, but I just couldn't piece together any more information. The Senate committee asserted that they could find the deposit of funds from Matthew McCloskey but did not find transfers of money to Bobby Baker, as my uncle had declared. That meant that as far as the documents were concerned, my uncle had stolen an overage. If that were true, that would be another felony, on top of the conspiracy to defraud the government on an overage, and stealing money from a friend's bank accounts in Nassau!

In addition to the mysteries that still needed solving, there were still so many people to contact. We tried to reach out to Robert Caro, but received no response. Left on the list was my ninety-five-year-old Aunt Jerry, who went through all of the tumult in 1963-1968; my third aunt's sister and her daughter, who knew something about my aunt and her involvement in the Baker scandal; Senate Historian Donald Ritchie, who interviewed Bobby Baker in his final visit to the Senate in 2009; Professor Robert Dallek, on his dubious pronouncement that LBJ had no connection to the Baker scandal; James Wagenvoord, the sole surviving member of the *Life* magazine newsroom, who attested that LBJ was going to prison just before President Kennedy's assassination; Professor KC Johnson, from State University of New York, who maintained that LBJ came close to obstruction of justice in the McCloskey affair; Professor

Carol Hofstetter, who wrote *Honest John Williams,* and mentioned my uncle as a key informer; Dan Beckman, whose father witnessed my uncle's farmhouse fire in Oakland, Maryland; and James Rada, the *Cumberland Gazette* news reporter who talked about my uncle's experiences with IRS agents on the streets in Oakland.

As tough as the remaining lists of interviews and mysteries were (on top of the stresses and complications of the ongoing COVID-19 pandemic) there was still cause for my hope with an event that occurred in 2021.

February 13, 2021 was a bitterly cold day in Madison, WI. I was out doing my rural postal route when I got stuck in a snowbank. While waiting for the tow truck, I returned a call to Archivist Greg Smith in Lodi, Wisconsin.

"Bob, I've got good news, and bad news," he said. "The FBI has located all the files on Don B. Reynolds … but it will cost you. The files contain over 17,000 pages."

I had to get back to work, so I told Greg I would speak with him later. I finished my route under tough winter conditions, but I was bolstered, knowing that this story had by no means ended. The hardship of my snowy route reminded me of the hardship I had faced writing this family memoir: at the end of the day, I would get there, but with a lot more effort that I expected!

On Monday, February 15, I confirmed with Greg that the 17,000 pages that were potentially responsive to the subject Don Buck Reynolds did not include any potential files from the IRS, CIA, and Pentagon. After discussing the twists and turns of the FOIA process, Greg pronounced that I did indeed have a great story and offered to go through half of the thirty-four CDs that the FBI would send. Printwise, the total was the equivalent of fifty, 350-page books.

Later, Greg wrote to me:

> Your timing is great. This is a story that *must be told* and *told by you.* You have my complete help and whatever I can do. I am so excited. We will have a lot to discern, but we can do it in good order and together. I am on board for the long haul. Thank you!

Now I wasn't alone. I had a copilot who was in it for the long haul! I hoped that we could not only tell history, but make history too.

Maybe no one had seen those FBI files in their entirety before. I was excited, but also a little scared about what could be in them.

Robert Caro was ordered by his boss to "turn every goddamned page" (so much so, that he made it his own motto) and as a result, he discovered that my uncle testified at the very same moment JFK was assassinated. Would it be the same for us as with Caro, that we would discover something earthshaking buried in those thirty-four CDs?

***

In March 2023, I reached out to Eric Parkinson, who, along with LBJ's attorney, Barr McClellan, had tried to tell their story. I told Eric I was contemplating contacting Luci Byrd Johnson to get her assessment of this memoir and her father's legacy. Eric said, "I wouldn't do that if I were you. By contacting Linda, you are essentially waving a red flag in front of yourself. I wouldn't be surprised if you get a cease-and-desist order."

He related that years ago, he and Barr were supposed to go on *Good Morning America,* but just hours before their appearance, they were informed that their spot had been cancelled. Later, he found out that LBJ's special assistant, Jack Valenti, had put pressure on the network to abandon the show.

***

Getting the story has turned into a story itself, and I realized that the shockwaves are still reverberating; they have shaped not only the landscape I'd already travelled, but the path that lay ahead of me as well.

***

I had lived in Madison since 2001, working at the University of Wisconsin Survey Center at Sterling Hall (the site of the Dow Chemical bombings). Sterling Hall is just a stone's throw away from the summit of Bascom Hill, with its commanding view of downtown Madison and the Capitol.

Working at the Survey Center, I had numerous opportunities to ponder two inscriptions that I found to be guiding lights. The famous plaque affixed to Bascom Hall firmly states, "Let it be known, that great state University of Wisconsin, encourages that fearless sifting and winnowing, by only which the truth can be known." And not far away, a statue of Abraham Lincoln extolls, "Let us believe that right makes might, and in that belief, dare to do our duty." The inspiring view from Bascom Hill was matched by the inspiring words.

Five months after the release of *The Guilty Men,* The History Channel aired a rebuttal on which Moderator Frank Sesno asked Professor Stanley Kutler about the enduring image of LBJ concerning corruption, and bribery.[1]

---

[1] YouTube: History Channel, *Response to the Guilty Men – an Historical Overview.* 41 minute

Kutler rolled his eyes and essentially said that there's always been corruption; it's hardly worth taking notice.

Professor Kutler's nonanswer is even more arresting when you consider his background in the Watergate scandal: he wrote the definitive work that forced Richard Nixon to release the tapes!

Where was the sifting and winnowing?

Certainly, an academic of Kutler's national caliber would be able to recognize the potential for impeachment that John Williams perceived – specifically from the documents that my uncle handed over – wouldn't he? Did he not know that Burkett Van Kirk said that LBJ would have been forced out? Did he not believe the insider Bobby Baker, a Democrat himself, when he said that Johnson might have suffered "a *mortal wound* from these revelations."[2] Sadly, it appears that some academics will not contribute to any understanding about the darker side of LBJ.

It was clear to me that someone else would have to sift and winnow. Someone else would have to believe that right makes might, and dare to do it. I am grateful that those words of wisdom, emblazoned in metal, spoke to me so personally and inspired me to embark on this journey.

I confided to my researcher and archivist, Greg Smith, that some people would perceive a partisan angle to this memoir, since the Baker scandal indeed pitted the Republicans against the Democrats. But once Greg understood the main points of this story, he remarked, "This doesn't concern political parties. It's not about politics. It's about right and wrong." So, let's sift and winnow in true Wisconsin tradition, and proceed with Lincoln's conviction that indeed, right makes might, and in that belief, we dare to do our duty.

---

mark to 43 minute mark
2   *The Passage of Power: The Years of Lyndon Johnson*, Robert Caro, page 47. https://bookreadfree.com/212449/5261605 & Caro, R. A. (2012, March 26). "The Transition." *The New Yorker*. https://www.newyorker.com/magazine/2012/04/02/the-transition-kennedy-assassination-lbj

From left to right: My Aunt Mary Lou, friend Dorothy Lambert, wife Ingrid Luttert, and Don Reynolds.

My family and I on vacation. There were always family get-togethers.

Introduction

In 1963, my Aunt Jerry persuaded my uncle to accept an offer from a famous senator to become a national star ... by becoming the Star Witness in a political scandal – a scandal that involved the President of the United States. Almost overnight, Uncle Buck achieved celebrity status and notoriety in the uproar called the "Bobby Baker Scandal." The History Channel, Walter Cronkite, Senate testimony on CBS, and numerous books followed.

The story of this Star Witness – my family's story – and the implications for the Senate, and most importantly, for LBJ's legacy, has never been fully told. How Don B. Reynolds crossed paths with Lyndon Baines Johnson, and Robert (Bobby) Gene Baker – particularly during the assassination of JFK – and survived, remains incredibly personal and mysterious.

There was not one, but two assassination attempts on November 22, 1963. One was tragically successful – ending the life of a beloved president – and the other was tragically not; the shots meant to end in political death were dodged by power and circumstance. That narrative is inextricably intertwined with my family's secrets. It is time those dodged shots finally find their mark.

There was the illegal act, and then the cover-up: my uncle was required to kickback advertising money and a stereo set to the Senate Majority Leader. He testified and LBJ mounted an attack via the press to smear and silence him. In the RFK stadium bond deal, my uncle showed illegal money flowing to the 1960 presidential campaign for Johnson. The President engineered a Senate cover-up, which still stands to this day. LBJ illegally used the FBI and IRS to abuse and intimidate my uncle, prevented a key witness, his aide Walter Jenkins from testifying, and coordinated answers regarding the McCloskey affair, which was a potential obstruction of justice.

Did these illegal acts have national consequences? Could they have lead to impeachment? Was it a scandal of Watergate proportions? The lead Senate investigator, John Williams, (Republican, Delaware) seemed to think so, and my uncle was his primary catalyst for getting the investigation started.

Pulitzer Prize-winning author, Robert Caro, discovered that my uncle testified against LBJ during President Kennedy's assassination. That was our family secret, kept for over 60 years. Our family, from personal experience, could honestly agree with the title of Victor Lasky's book *It didn't start with Watergate*. There was no Watergate for LBJ, but over a period of sixty years, evidence has accumulated from a wide variety of sources that proves the Baker scandal was indeed the LBJ scandal!

> Historically, it seemed as if President Lyndon Baines Johnson, could make anything happen. The tall Texan was a larger-than-life politician; he spearheaded Medicare, signed the Civil Rights Act, envisioned the Great Society, and stood behind the debacle of Vietnam. He was probably the greatest Senate Majority Leader in U.S. history. Yet, given his outsized ego, it also wouldn't be a stretch to think he could be involved in some kind of wrongdoing, in this case, a scandal: The Bobby Baker Scandal, aptly named by the press and spanning from 1963-1967.[3]

Baker was a Senate employee, LBJ's trusted vote counter who helped him pass critical legislation in the '50s and early '60s. LBJ famously said that Baker was "the first person [he saw] in the morning and the last person [he saw] at night."[4]

In 1967, Baker went to jail for his transgressions, but LBJ wasn't touched. There were hints of LBJ's involvement, but certainly no calls for impeachment – at worst, he was only guilty of indirect involvement.

And where did my Uncle Buck fit into this picture?

My mother's brother, Donald Buck Reynolds, was an insurance broker, and the business partner and longtime friend of Bobby Baker, the Secretary to the Senate Democratic Majority. Through Baker's connections, Uncle Buck wrote life insurance on the Senate Majority Leader in the '50s and the Vice President in the early '60s. Then, after Bobby Baker himself was enmeshed in scandal in October 1963, my uncle was drawn into the spotlight, primarily through three separate business transactions with LBJ.

But there was a redeeming and heroic element to my uncle's story: he decided to come clean and blow the whistle. He set a day to testify to the Senate Rules Committee.

---

3   Taking Charge, The Johnson White House Tapes, Simon and Schuster, Michael Beschloss, p. 187
4   https://www.washingtonpost.com/local/obituaries/bobby-baker-protege-of-lyndon-johnson-felled-by-influence-peddling-scandal-dies-at-89/2017/11/17/ffb7ce04-cc06-11e7-b0cf-7689a9f2d84e_story.html (accessed 6/13/24)

CHAPTER ONE

WHAT STARTED IT ALL
NOVEMBER 22, 1963

So is 2020 the worst year ever? For the young among us today, the answer is no doubt yes. But, for many of us, this day in 1963 still seems like it started it all.
– Dave Zweifel, *Wisconsin Capital Times*

It was November 22, 1963.

The sky was grey and slightly foreboding, but the temperature was warmer than expected. There was still a chill in the air, but it wasn't the biting cold that was common during the winter months in Washington, D.C. Thanksgiving was less than a week away and the anticipation of time off and family visits was palpable.

One man didn't have the impending holidays on his mind; he had come to Washington for a very specific reason. He was a little anxious but he didn't show it. His large frame exuded confidence and control. Donald Buck Reynolds climbed the tapering steps to the Russell Senate Office Building. Its design in marble and limestone subtly echoed the Capitol; he felt the weight of what he was about to do bearing down on him.

I knew Donald Buck Reynolds simply as Uncle Buck, but because he was making his way to a tiny room in the Old Senate Office Building on that fateful day, he was going to be known to the world as "The Star Witness." He entered the room and sat down at the solitary table. Across from him were Republican Minority Lead Counsel Clayton Burkett Van Kirk, and Lorin Drennan, an accountant from the Government Accounting Office.

Uncle Buck set his briefcase down and unsnapped the metal clasp. He felt the leather under his fingers for a moment before fully opening the case and pulling out stacks of paper. Careully, he laid out the documents that he believed implicated the sitting Vice President, and he started to talk.

Van Kirk and Drennan were so fascinated by Uncle Buck's testimony that they ordered in sandwiches, so they could continue to listen nonstop.

***

At that very same moment, in Texas, President Kennedy's car, rolling slowly in the Dallas motorcade, was approaching the Texas Book Depository. At 12:30 PM Central Time. shots rang out. Chaos and fear, sadness, and disbelief erupted.

***

Back in Washington, the Senate investigators had forgotten that my uncle, Van Kirk, and Drennan were in that small office; my uncle kept talking. At 3:30 in the afternoon [Eastern Time], a secretary burst into the room. Tears were streaming down her cheeks as she sobbed that President Kennedy had been fatally shot, and Lyndon Johnson was about to be sworn in as the thirty-sixth President of the United States.

Everything fell silent and still for an eternal moment.... The President had been slain. The enormity of it stunned Uncle Buck but almost immediately, he could feel the small hairs rise at the nape of his neck. He felt off balance; the room had transformed into the small cabin of a seagoing vessel and seemed to pitch from left to right and back again. He loosened his tie just a touch and took a deep breath. A weight had settled on his chest, and he felt a bead of sweat forming at the edge of his hairline. He tried to breathe deeply again, but it was harder this time. He had just testified against the Vice President ... who was now about to be the President of the United States. History had overtaken my uncle – personally and directly.

The tumult inside him was never betrayed by his countenance. He steadied himself and managed to find his breath again. He was back at the helm – but the voyage had changed course dramatically. He thought to himself, with no small sense of wonder, that he had, in effect, just politically assassinated the newly sworn-in President; the evidence he had provided was enough to force LBJ to resign or be impeached.

He paused for a final moment and settled himself in his decision. He reached for the incriminating documents that littered the table, and said that the Rules Committee wouldn't need them now. "Giving testimony involving the Vice President is one thing, but when it involves the President himself, that is something else. You can just forget that I ever said anything if you want to."[5] He said it quietly but firmly.

---

[5] *Despoilers of Democracy,* Clark Mollenhoff, Doubleday & Company, 1965 p.299

"Too late," said Van Kirk; the documents were in the custody of the Senate Rules Committee.

Later that day, my uncle returned to his office despite being unable to work; his mind swam with every possible trajectory that he might now find himself on.

Uncle Buck and the author, his "favorite nephew"

Uncle Buck and my mother.

CHAPTER TWO

THE END OF FAMILY SECRETS
APRIL 2019

It was 10:30 PM on April 29, 2019, when my wife took the call at our home in DeForest, a village north of Madison. It was my mom's home health nurse. "I'm sorry," she said, "She's gone."

At 96, my mother, Uncle Buck's sister, Connie Reynolds Nelson, peacefully left this earth. One week prior, her sister-in-law, my aunt Ingrid Reynolds (Uncle Buck's third wife) had also taken her last breath. With those two deaths, the motivation for writing a family memoir about my mother's infamous brother, Don Buck Reynolds – the man one author called "the final spark to the crime of the century"[6] – had ironically been given new life.

In our family, talk about the scandal was seldom heard. We just wanted to forget it. In 2017, my mother and I were driving from Madison, Wisconsin to our hometown in Munster, Indiana. I mentioned casually that Bobby Baker had recently passed away. "Oh?" she said. Then she reflected, "It was too bad about Buck. Got in with the wrong people I guess … You know, they never did find out the cause of his farmhouse fire…"

Even when my Aunt Ingrid came to visit at our home in DeForest in 2018, I couldn't find the courage to ask her any questions about the scandal. I wanted to know more, but it seemed so rude and impolite to broach the subject. *Was I a reporter or her beloved nephew?*

After my mother passed, I cleaned out her apartment. While doing so, I discovered a letter that my uncle's second wife had written to her in February of 1964. It was regarding the scandal, and me. The end of the letter said, "[Don's] fighting like mad to make this a better world for Bobby. I hope he'll understand one day."

That letter was sixty years old. It prompted a number of questions. *Did my uncle succeed? Was it a better world? How could I understand – by asking relatives, reading, having a gut feeling?*

Reaching for Glory, White House Tapes. Bechloss, p. 203

Chicago Tribune headline showing the danger my uncle faced. Our family kept a scrapbook of my uncle's travails.

CHAPTER THREE

LBJ's Crisis In Copenhagen

October 1963

In 1962 and early 1963, the United States was top dog in the world. The economy was roaring, there was international respect, a telegenic and admired president was at the helm. What could go wrong?

For the Vice President, things started to change for the worse during a state visit with the Danish king and queen in Copenhagen after he received a transatlantic call from his trusted administrative aide, Walter Jenkins. Jenkins had discovered a lawsuit against Bobby Baker filed by Ralph Hill of South Carolina.

Johnson was scheduled to enjoy a festive evening at the Tivoli Gardens in downtown Copenhagen. As one of the oldest amusement parks in the world, its main purpose was to delight and amuse, but despite the lighthearted atmosphere, LBJ had the sword of Damocles suspended above him, and he knew it. LBJ was panicking (as described by his press secretary, George Reedy). The Texan was usually the one to make others panic with his "LBJ treatment," but now the tables had turned, and he knew this could be the beginning of the end for his long political career.

On October 6, my Uncle Buck entered the picture by way of the *Herald Tribune*; he had been talking, and the *Tribune* picked it up. The trail of info went from GOP Strategist Phil Brennan, to businessman Ralph Hill, then to Senator John Williams. Then, Hill recommended that Senator Williams contact my uncle. That's when my uncle "spilled his guts" (as Bobby Baker put it) to the Delaware senator.

Once back in Washington, Johnson flipped through the national newspapers, as was his daily custom. According to Earl Deathe, LBJ's assistant at his ranch, Johnson knew this would be trouble. He had gotten things that he had not paid for, and my uncle knew his secrets. Receiving kickbacks was a charge that could spell the end for a politician. As if that weren't enough, an even bigger juggernaut was aimed at the Vice President.

Life Magazine had loaded a missile, and its target was LBJ. James Wagenvoord, a veteran of *Life Magazine* shared his experiences from 1963:

> I was the 27-year-old Editorial business manager and assistant to *Life Magazine's* Executive Editor. Beginning in later summer 1963 the magazine, based upon information fed from Bobby Kennedy and the Justice Department, had been developing a major newsbreak piece concerning Johnson and Bobby Baker. On publication Johnson would have been finished and off the '64 ticket (reason the material was fed to us) and would probably have been facing prison time. At the time *Life Magazine* was arguably the most important general news source in the US. The top management of Time Inc. was closely allied with the USA's various intelligence agencies, and we were used by the Kennedy Justice Department as a conduit to the public. *Life*'s coverage of the Hoffa prosecution, and involvement in paying off Justice Department Memphis witnesses was a case in point.[7]

(I met Wagenvoord first in Dallas at an assassination conference in November 2019, and later at his home in Yardley, Pennsylvania during my first trip to Delaware in January 2020. He was the only surviving person from that newsroom. He had a wealth of knowledge, and it seemed as if he really wanted to divulge as much as possible.)

On October 7, 1963, a meeting was called by Senate Majority Leader Mike Mansfield to address some of the charges about Baker. Baker did not attend and the Secretary to the Senate Majority resigned.

At that time, I was blissfully unaware of any of these developments, and if my mom knew, she didn't tell me. The Beatles had recorded "I Want to Hold Your Hand" on October 17; what could be more important to a young kid?

In Washington, the political heat was on. Which investigation would gain traction first? Which one would do the most, lasting damage to the Vice President?

In the end, neither found its mark. Why?

---

[7] "*Life* Magazine, LBJ and the Assassination of JFK," John Simkin. https://educationforum.ipbhost.com/topic/14966-life-magazine-lbj-and-the-assassination-of-jfk/

CHAPTER FOUR

FAMILY HISTORY, ASSASSINATION, AND A STAR WITNESS

I guess you won't need these. Giving testimony involving the Vice President is one thing, but when it involves the President himself, that is something else. You can just forget that I ever said anything if you want to.[8]

–My Uncle to Senate investigators,
Washington, D.C. November 22, 1963

When I attended the fiftieth anniversary of the JFK assassination in 2013, I bought a three-by-two foot poster from the Sixth Floor Museum at Dealey Plaza. It shows an admiring throng, Secret Service agents looking intently at the crowds, a prominently displayed "All the Way with JFK" sign, and the Continental limo turning onto Main Street in Dallas – the President and Jackie in the third row of seats and Nellie and John Connally in the second. At the bottom of the poster, Glen Gatlin, a motorcade spectator, wrote, "You had a feeling that you were a part of an important national event – something that might even be a bit historic."

Whenever I gaze into that photo and echo Gatlin's comment, I think about my family and my uncle as they were at that very moment in time. They were not in the motorcade, but the Reynolds-Nelson clan was a part of that historic event.

***

Culturally, it was quite the jump from a small tobacco town in South Carolina to the nation's capital, but that didn't matter to Don Reynolds; he had always been headed for bigger and brighter days.

He was born in 1915, into a family of nine, and raised in the southern crucible pre-Civil Rights era. His parents named him Chapel Lee. (My mom said he hated that name so as soon as he was able, he went to the courthouse to change it.) Two of his siblings died in infancy, and an-

---

Despoilers of Democracy, Clark Mollenhoff, Doubleday & Company, 1965 p. 299.

other, my Uncle William, died in a swimming accident at age nineteen at Lake Lure, North Carolina. My grandfather collapsed after taking the call announcing his son's death. That left six young people in my mother's family.

Growth and success had always been on Uncle Buck's mind. My mom said, "While all the other boys were playing, your uncle was hitting the books. I would see him outside, back up against the wall of the house, reading history – particularly military history." In 1939, Uncle Buck left all his memories of small-town southern life and got an appointment to the U.S. Military Academy.

Uncle Buck wasn't the only determined one. His siblings also made it to the big time. My Aunt Mary Lou, the sister closest to Uncle Buck, received advanced training in theology at Scarritt College for Christian Workers in Nashville and became the director of the American Red Cross in Augusta, Georgia. For her service, she received a tribute in the Congressional Record.

His other sister, my Aunt Genevieve, became a society writer for the *Washington Post*. She knew presidents and prime ministers, and in a letter to my aunt, she warned that my uncle's challenging LBJ was a fool's errand. She was a perfect example of the small-town girl who went to the big city and showed them how to do it.

> [Genevieve] Reynolds, a Darlington County native, wanted an interview with Generalissimo Chiang Kai-shek, the Nationalist Chinese leader, but Chinese officials told her that Chiang was too busy. Besides they said, he never, ever granted interviews to women journalists.[9]

Aunt Genevieve bet a colleague $100 that she would succeed in getting an audience with the generalissimo. She grabbed her notebook and headed for Chiang's headquarters. She landed the interview. When she told Chiang about the bet, he laughed. "Young lady," he said, "The next time you make that bet, make it a big one."

Early on, my mom wanted to be a teacher, but she was also blessed with other talents. She was third for the state in the 1942 *Miss America* pageant. When my dad met my mom during basic training in Columbia, South Carolina, he couldn't help but take notice of her. The rest is history.

After my parents married, they moved to Madison and my dad attended the University of Wisconsin on the GI Bill. In 1960, my father was

---

[9] November 23, 2000, lifestyle page of the *Darlington News and Press*

transferred from Madison back to Chicago, and we settled down in the bedroom community of Munster, Indiana, twenty-five miles from Chicago.

Munster was a good choice, and if it was good for me, it was especially wonderful for my dad: he had escaped an alcoholic father and an abusive childhood, and he was able to comfortably settle down with his family. The school system was excellent, and both my mom and dad had good jobs. Gas was twenty-nine cents a gallon and land was cheap – in 1963, we built our new home on Jefferson Avenue.

I was an only child, the apple of my parents' eyes, and rightly or wrongly, the center of my family's attention. Everything seemed placid and perfect, like sailing across a calm lake. It was a *Leave-It-To-Beaver* life! Our bulwarks were the safe community, a great school, the local church, and a strong, two-parent family. The world was at peace, and the economy was strong – the wind was at our backs.

I spent a number of summers with my Uncle Buck and Aunt Jerry at their new home in Silver Spring, Maryland, a suburb of D.C., and also at their farmhouse in Oakland, Maryland. I remember swimming and boating at Deep Creek Lake; their two, adorable German shepherds, Renni and Penni; and the hearty breakfasts my aunt would prepare at the farmhouse during those idyllic country summers. It seemed like *Theme from a Summer Place*. Every Fourth of July, my uncle would buy a prodigious amount of fireworks, then blast them off from the small hill at his property on Venetian Road in Silver Spring. We had a great time. When I spent my summers with them, I didn't sense any tension or marital trouble.

The summer of 1963 passed with such great memories, and in the fall, you could hear "The Lazy, Hazy, Crazy Days of Summer," "Surf City," and "He's So Fine" on the hit parade. My dad, being a rabid UW football fan, traversed the 150 miles on Saturday from Munster to Madison to watch the Badgers play at Camp Randall. We had just come off a championship 1962 season and were anticipating another great season.... Politics was the furthest thing from my mind. Yet, lying just below the surface, there were unseen problems: the Cuban Missile Crisis had just occurred (in Munster, just two miles from our home, there was a defensive underground Nike missile base), the Cold War was at its height, and Civil Rights were about to take center stage.

Unbeknownst to me, our family was about to be thrown into history. And as a ten-year-old kid, November 22, 1963 started out like just another school day. Before leaving our house to walk to Eads Elementary School,

I noticed a *Chicago Tribune* lying unfurled on the front stoop; the headline read, "Texas Crowds Greet Kennedy."

At school, we were in our free reading hour when it happened. At about 2:30 PM, our fifth grade teacher, Walter Olds, told us to put our books away – he had an announcement. Voice measured but somber, he intoned, "Class, President Kennedy went to Dallas, Texas and was travelling in a motorcade this afternoon. He was shot, taken to a hospital, and died."

It took our breath away.

Class was dismissed.

The Main Event had happened. What I didn't know was that Uncle Buck had already become The Star Witness. That very day, he had produced something worthy for the history books.

By sharing his evidence on November 22, 1963, Don Reynolds had unknowingly entered a very serious national political drama. He dared to speak truth to power. He dared to testify against the Vice President of the United States at the very minute the President was assassinated.

That made my uncle a problem, a big problem. It became a political boxing match: Uncle Buck, a Southern "hick" against Lyndon Johnson, the most powerful man in the world. Surely, Don Buck Reynolds, Maryland broker, would in due time, receive his own special version of "The LBJ Treatment."

***

I believe my uncle had three primary reasons to come forward: opportunity, personal motivation, and powerful support.

The financial and economic firewalls surrounding the Baker mess were beginning to collapse. In August of 1963, GOP Strategist Phil Brennan counseled Southern Carolina businessman, Ralph Hill, to talk with Delaware Senator John Williams regarding Hill's business problems. (Williams had a reputation for being a fair but relentless investigator of corruption.) Hill felt he had been double-crossed by Bobby Baker in his financial dealings with a Virginia company called Melpar regarding their food vending operations. During their conversations, my uncle's name came up repeatedly. (Hill even related my uncle's participation in a call girl ring, "Reynolds is in on it. The girls get $50, and they have to give back $20.")[10]

Soon after, Senator Williams called my uncle in for private consultations. My Aunt Jerry urged him to cooperate. She was tired of life in the

---

[10] *Despoilers of Democracy: The real story of what Washington propagandists, arrogant bureaucrats, mismanagers, influence peddlers, and outright corrupters are doing to our Federal Government* (1965), Doubleday, p. 275-277.

fast lane. As Pulitzer Prize-winning author, Clark Mollenhoff, wrote, "She didn't like the night life, the gay parties, the weekend trips to Miami and New York."[11]

My uncle came to like Senator Williams and appreciated his straightforward way of doing investigations. Eventually, Senator Williams became like a priest, a father confessor for Uncle Buck. In one of the letters that I collected at the University of Delaware, Senator Williams shared what my uncle had confessed to him:

> He described parties he had attended at the Carroll Arms which Mr. Reynolds described as "sex orgies" attended by Baker, Reynolds, and sometimes others at which time they would have their girls and enter the game of change partners.
> These sex orgies took place in New York, Washington, Miami, and elsewhere, and it seemed that it was the same group chasing around.[12]

Paul Aguirre, another Bobby Baker pal, typified the attitude of the people that my uncle associated with when he said, "My wife is expecting a denial, and she's going to get it. I don't care if they have photographs. I'll take the first to the twenty-eighth amendments."

Major McLendon, the lead counsel in the Baker scandal, once remarked, "I have heard that Mrs. Reynolds is an exceptional individual." As her nephew, I would agree. Actually, mere longsuffering in the face of this sexual frolicking doesn't do her justice. In a sense, Aunt Jerry was the proximate cause of the revealing of the national scandal of the '60s. Without her urging and calming presence, I don't think my uncle would have come forward.

My uncle also had support from Robert Kennedy, who had already taken action against prominent Democrats in various states. The only chance to bring down Lyndon Johnson lay in the investigation crossing Robert Kennedy's desk so that he could force Johnson to resign, or assign prosecutors to charge him with criminal activities and have the FBI back it up with all the evidence needed for conviction. This situation required the full weight of the Justice Department, with the sympathies and backing of the American public, to see it through. I imagine having the U.S. Justice Department at my uncle's back was indeed comforting.

So, on the morning of November 22, 1963, my uncle drove the twenty miles from Silver Spring to Washington DC, staunchly ascended the

---

11   Ibid, p. 294
12   Senator Williams. University of Delaware Archives, Collection

steps of Capitol Hill, and told his story to the Senate investigators in the Old Senate office building. Clark Mollenhoff related that some individuals had promised my uncle big trouble, but he remained firm in his desire to testify and come clean.

Burkett Van Kirk, Republican Minority lead counsel said:

> Don presented a good case. He could back it up. Everything he said he had a receipt for. It's hard to argue with a receipt, a cancelled check, or an invoice. It's hard to argue with documentation. LBJ had no idea that as Kennedy was shot, Reynolds was handing over evidence the Republicans hoped to use to impeach him.[13]

Van Kirk stated that he withheld the news about the shooting for fear that my uncle would clam up. Other reports said that no one knew my uncle and the Republican members of the Rules Committee were there on Capitol Hill, and when a crying secretary burst into the room, the testimony was adjourned.

My uncle had awoken that morning at 7:00 AM, and by 3:30 PM, not only had he testified, but the events in Dallas had changed everything. He drove back to Silver Spring, Maryland, shaken to his core. He had, at a defining point in U.S. history, in executive session, given credible information against the thirty-sixth President of the United States of America.

In Dallas, the new Commander-in-Chief definitely knew about my uncle and the ramifications of his testimony on December 22, 1963. One of the first phone calls LBJ made after the assassination, aboard Air Force One, was to his attorney, Abe Fortas. "What did Reynolds say?" was his concerned query.

***

Robert Caro said:

> It's almost unbelievably dramatic in terms of the time sequence. ... nobody had connected LBJ to the Bobby Baker scandal. At the very moment that morning, back in Washington, in a closed little room in the Senate office building, the man who was going to connect Johnson to that scandal, a man named Don Reynolds, was testifying before Senate investigators.
>
> And he was pushing across the table to them the checks and the invoice that would prove that LBJ was involved in the Baker scandal, which was the huge scandal of that time. He was doing this at approximately the time that the motorcade was going through

---

[13] *Chasing Demons* on Vimeo.

Dallas and the shots rang out.[14]

Author Ron Rosenbaum wrote about his interview with Caro in which he related his discovery:

> Caro's narrative has an astonishing reminder of how close the investigation of Bobby Baker came to bringing LBJ down. In fact, until now, Caro believes, no one has put together just what a close call it was.
> ... *Life* had an investigative SWAT team on the case!
> The Senate had a subcommittee taking testimony about kickbacks and extortion Baker engaged in on LBJ's behalf while he was Vice President. The kind of thing that got Spiro Agnew kicked out of the vice presidency. It was in reading this testimony that Caro made a remarkable discovery.
> ..."A thousand books on the assassination," Caro says, "and I don't know of one that realizes that at that very moment Lyndon Johnson's world was to come crashing down, Reynolds is giving them these documents."
> Caro still gets excited talking about his discovery.
> "Oh, it's great. ... Nobody writes this," he says. "Bobby Baker says the thing I quote in the book, 'If I had talked it would have inflicted a mortal wound on LBJ.' And it starts coming out – and stops coming out – just as JFK receives his mortal wound in Dallas.
> "... The counsel to the Rules Committee says, 'So you started testifying what time?' And [Reynolds] says, 'Ten o'clock.' That's on November 22. He was testifying while President Kennedy was being shot!"[15]

Caro was so excited about something our family had known for fifty years!

My uncle's testimony proved that LBJ had demanded and accepted kickbacks, primarily through a stereo, and ad time on his Texas station KTBC in Austin; and, later to be fully revealed, exposed that a campaign slush fund had been engineered to benefit the 1960 LBJ presidential campaign.

If that weren't enough, *Life Magazine* had eight or nine reporters combing the LBJ Ranch and asking pertinent questions regarding LBJ's fortune. How a public official earning $25,000 a year had accumulated $13,000,000 in fifteen years deserved some attention!

James Wagenvoord of *Life* stated that during assassination week, there had been two articles on the Baker scandal already published, but nothing

---

14   NPR, *Fresh Air*, Dave Davies, February 20, 2023
15   "Should LBJ Be Ranked Alongside Lincoln?," Ron Rosenbaum, *Smithsonian*, May 2012.

linking LBJ directly to the scandal. The third issue *would* have been published two days after the assassination. "It was all coming from Bobby, we had him. LBJ would have been out and facing prison time. It was coming from the Justice Department," related Wagenvoord.

Then, at the 2020 CAPA (Committee of Associations on Political Assassinations) conference, he gave more information regarding the threat to LBJ, "I asked my boss Phil Wootten, 'How can you spike this story on LBJ?' Wootton replied, 'Jim, *we can't kill two presidents in twenty-four hours.*'" The *Life* story was subsequently shredded, but Wagenvoord added that RFK kept a copy for his own use during the 1968 campaign. When Wagenvoord and his wife went out to dinner, he conveyed his sense of disappointment and vented with his colleagues that a man like LBJ had taken control of the government reins.

The big guns of *Life* had fallen silent, and the other main source of political intelligence, Bobby Baker, took the Fifth Amendment. That left the testimony of one man, my uncle, against the most powerful man in the world. My uncle's testimony did have the capacity to leave a "mortal wound" – not physically, but on LBJ's presidential record and legacy.

How would LBJ, the Senate, and Bobby Baker react? Would the truth be found, or would there be a massive cover up engineered to try to protect larger-than-life Lyndon's legacy?

CHAPTER FIVE

A Family In The Spotlight & Private Presidential Panic

December 1963-March 1964

The things that make me so proud ... is that Don is fighting for principles. He's been just wonderful, he's not too tense, and he's fighting like mad to make this a better world for Bobby.
— Letter from my Aunt Jerry to my mom, February 1964

In December of 1963, the assassination was fresh in my mind, but the scandal was having a different kind of impact on our family. My uncle was not only involved, but throwing out multiple accusations. Picking a fight with a powerful political figure is not something one does every day on a whim!

Despite the *Chicago Tribune* being delivered daily to our house, I remained blissfully unaware of my uncle's testimony. My parents adopted a nothing-to-see-here strategy. Even though the events were so close to home, they remained shrouded in mystery and fog. My mom and dad tried very hard to put a protective shield around their only child. One of their motivations was, well, the sexual angle. If I had started reading the *Tribune*, national magazines, or any other publications, at some point, I was bound to come across all the call girl, abortion, and who-was-sharing-a-bed-with-whom stories. It was *National Enquirer* material as well as national security material.

(Later, my father offered me some off-the-cuff advice about career. He talked about the difference between government and business – he had chosen the latter. "Bob," he said, "If you chose to work for the government, the security and benefits are good, but you're not going to become wealthy, at least not legally." As if to make sure his son fully understood what the family had experienced with Bobby Baker, he took a dramatic pause: "Son, if you work for the government – *stay out of scandal.*"

I never forgot it, and looking back, I could understand the impact that the Baker scandal, and later Watergate, had made on my dad. My moralistic streak, my aversion to getting into any kind of ethical or legal dilemmas, has remained strong throughout my entire life – perhaps overly so.)

***

Then there was LBJ. There were rumors that he had stolen a Senate election in 1948 (which earned him the derisive nickname "Landslide Lyndon"), and that he was on the verge of destruction with *Life Magazine* and my uncle. Now, due to the seminal event in our nation's history, my uncle had privately accused the President of the United States of political corruption.

***

In early December 1963, after arriving home from school, my mom promptly announced a pleasant surprise: my Uncle Buck was at a motel in the nearby city of Hammond, Indiana, and we'd all be going out to dinner together. For me, it was a real treat, but the motivations and actions of adults are often kept underground and are not readily apparent to a ten-year-old. In truth, after testifying, my uncle was trying to get out of the political heat of Washington, D.C.

At around 6:00 PM, my dad drove us in our AMC Rambler and picked up my uncle. On the way into the south side of Chicago, via the Dan Ryan (I-94) expressway, my uncle was unassuming and matter-of-fact. Much to the chagrin of my parents, he talked about John Profumo, the UK Secretary of State for War, and Christine Keeler, the nineteen-year-old model and call girl who had brought him down in a recent sex scandal. Maybe it was due to Uncle Buck's military training, or just his personality, but nothing in his tone of voice or mannerism indicated that he was agitated or in fear of his life. And yet, there was still no doubt that during that dark, cold December night, things were somewhat amiss.

On his drive west from Washington, my uncle had signed hotel registers "Don Buck" so as to throw off anyone trying to trace his whereabouts, and before going into the restaurant, we all agreed that his assumed name for the night would be "Charlie."

We sat down, looked at the menu, and decided what to order. "Charlie," my dad said with the dutiful seriousness of a budding actor, "what will you have?"

After the waiter collected all of our orders and left, I committed the one and only serious faux pas of the evening. "Uncle Buck," I said in a not-so-soft voice, "What do you think..."

"Shhhh! There could be agents over there," said my uncle in a hushed tone, glancing over at the nearby table.

Despite the tense moment, we were still able to enjoy the rest of our evening together, just more cautiously so. Later, my dad navigated the streets of Chicago back to Munster, taking streets he thought the Feds wouldn't know. It was all so entertaining to me at the time; it was like cops and robbers, James Bond ... certainly, a change from my fifth grade schoolwork at Eads!

Even years later, my uncle wouldn't let me live down that incident at the dinner table. Considering all he had been through, and having worked in Air Force Intelligence, I could certainly understand his reaction. He didn't trust the FBI, or anything that the LBJ administration could throw his way.

My uncle took great efforts to evade the FBI. After his testimony, he was travelling across the country by train. The agents were closing in. In retelling the story, my mom exclaimed, "I tell you, when those FBI agents boarded the train and started opening compartment doors, Buck started speaking Spanish so fast to the woman sitting next to him!" She laughed and laughed. Honestly, I couldn't help but join in the rare mirth amidst such a serious national scandal.

My uncle left the next morning; we wished him well. Life in Munster would revert back to regular daily rhythms – or so we thought. Unfortunately, we soon learned that we were not immune from the long reach of D.C. politics. As we tried to go about our normal lives, we were forcibly thrown into the drama.

On a cold January day, with snow obscuring vision to fifty feet, my mother and I drove into the garage after school. (My mom was a teacher at the same elementary school I attended, and we would sometimes come home together). We commiserated that nobody should be out in this mess. We were glad to get back home. No sooner had my mom shut off the engine, when she said the words I'll never forget, "Here they come, Bob." I looked back from the car and saw two men with black coats and hats fighting their way through the blowing snow to our garage.

We got out of the car and faced two FBI agents. The polite but direct question posed to my mom was if we knew the recent whereabouts of a man named Don B. Reynolds. My mom turned to me to help answer. "We haven't seen him recently, have we Bob?"

"No, no," I responded.

(The place where I stood in the garage, my mom's tone of voice, and the look and mannerisms of the two men are all so indelibly imprinted in my mind. Over sixty years later, I can recall it as clearly as the day it happened.)

The men didn't carry visible guns, they wished us no harm, and they were respectful, but children instinctively know when something is out of the ordinary; it was clear that those FBI agents weren't out in the blowing and drifting snow for some menial reason.

Later, I would discover that LBJ had ordered a full field investigation of my uncle, which included family, friends, and acquaintances. Before that snowy day with the FBI, government officials were working behind the scenes to limit the damage of Uncle Buck's November 22 testimony. They would be back to Munster more times than we could imagine.

My dad related a story to me about a car that was parked in the same spot near our house, day after day. Finally, in exasperation, he walked up to the car and said to the man inside, "Don't you think it's a waste of taxpayer money to watch a ten-year-old child go to school every day?"

***

On December 6, 1963, Uncle Buck received a call from LBJ's press secretary, George Reedy (the same George Reedy who said that if LBJ just calmly explained everything, instead of panicking, there wouldn't be any problems for him in the Baker scandal). Reedy advised my uncle that it would "be best to refrain from making any more statements about Bobby Baker and LBJ." Later, Reedy lamely claimed the call was just a reminder that Uncle Buck's clients would not want to do business with him if he continued to make such proclamations.

In a taped telephone conversation with Reedy in early January, LBJ ordered Reedy to contact *Time, Newsweek,* and the *Washington Post,* to put pressure on them to stop printing adverse stories on the affidavit that vice presidential aide, Walter Jenkins, had submitted. The affidavit was crafted by Major Lennox Polk McLendon (counsel for the Senate Rules Committee) to protect not just Jenkins, but LBJ as well. It was in direct conflict with my uncle's testimony. The affidavit reminded me of something my uncle said: "*They answer their own questions*" – they pick the questions to ensure that the answers to those questions exculpate the actual wrongdoers. Caro indeed said that LBJ had a "bottomless capacity for deceit."

LBJ appointed Everett Jordan, the senator from North Carolina, as chairman of the Senate Rules Committee investigating Bobby Baker. On December 9, 1963 Jordan called LBJ.

"They've got this receipt for the stereo," he said. Jordan indicated that he was doing all he could. "They won't get anything from Everett.... No, I don't want it spread; it might spread where we don't want it to spread. Mighty hard to put out a fire once it's been started."

As the nation celebrated the New Year on January 1, 1964, the Baker scandal was coming to a political boiling point. On January 10, in a telephone conversation to his advisors, LBJ said J. Edgar Hoover had already given him the FBI file on Reynolds. The new president said the problem was "there wasn't a goddamn thing to indict him on."

On January 9 and 17, my uncle testified to the Senate Rules Committee in a closed session. Then, Congress voted to release that information publicly. It created a sensation. The *New York Times* reported on January 21, "The Democratic members are believed to be wary about looking too deeply into areas that impinge upon the relationship between Mr. Baker and the President." Options were beginning to disappear for LBJ.

Senator Robert Byrd, Democrat of West Virginia, asked my uncle if Senator Johnson knew at the time the phonograph was installed that my uncle was the man who had given it to him.

Uncle Buck replied, "I don't think there would have been any question about it, sir, because, [for] this set, the invoice was billed from the Magnavox Company directly to Senator Johnson."

"But that would not necessarily connect you with the transaction," Senator Byrd said.

"It showed that the charges were to be sent to Don Reynolds, sir," Uncle Buck replied.

The political cat was out of the bag: there was a link between Don Reynolds and President Johnson – a connection to the Baker scandal!

On January 22, during a telephone conversation to Everett Jordan, Johnson said, "Just hope we have the votes on them." (Democrats held a 6-3 edge on the Rules Committee investigation.) LBJ anticipated that the Senate Democrats would shut down any further inquiry. He also made it clear that he would stop Walter Jenkins from testifying; "I'd just defy them," he said.

The only people that could resolve the conflict were Bobby Baker (who took the Fifth Amendment 120 times), and Walter Jenkins (who refused to testify and was allowed to submit an indistinct and unclear statement).

Jenkins was not allowed to be cross-examined to resolve the conflicting stories. One day before his scheduled appearance, two psychiatrists were called in to give their expert opinions that providing testimony would "kill him." The reason? Supposedly: the stress. Interestingly, the psychiatrists' notes were never found. (All along, my uncle asserted that Jenkins had received favorable treatment and should have been brought before the committee.)

On January 23, (on the advice of his attorney, Abe Fortas, to tell his side of the story) Johnson called a press conference and said the stereo was a gift from the Baker family. This, of course, was false; the invoice was sent to Don Reynolds, not Bobby Baker. Johnson left the conference quickly, not taking any questions. The press was not convinced; they could spot the presidential duplicity from miles away.

Then, on January 27, 1964, a remarkable conversation took place. It was recorded on the now-famous "I'm going to jail" tape. (It was mentioned by both Walter Pincus of the *Washington Post* and Michael Beschloss, who compiled an exhaustive list of LBJ tapes.) All the president's men: Jack Valenti, Bill Moyers, Walter Jenkins, and Abe Fortas, were present for the discussion.

(A contributor to the online Reynolds/LBJ forum, Joe Bauer, said that the hushed tones of the recording reminded him of Watergate with Colson, Haldeman, and Ehrlichman.)

In the conspiratorial taped dialogue, LBJ, concerned with my uncle's testimony, admitted his fear of going to jail. Talking to his attorney, Fortas, he said, "I don't want to go against your advice – because you have to defend me and if I don't do what you tell me, I'll be in a hell of a shape – but if I do, I'm going to jail. That's just how I see it." (LBJ regretted telling "his side" of the story at the press conference the day before. He believed the story that my uncle gave about the ad time and stereo kickbacks could eventually destroy his presidency, and probably, with other violations, send him to prison.)

On February 4, Johnson's blood pressure must have reached critical levels as more jail talk ensued. In the book *The Washington Pay-Off*, lobbyist Robert Winter Berger recalled LBJ's outbursts about the Baker scandal in Speaker John McCormick's office.

> LBJ was shouting, "John, that son of bitch [Bobby Baker] is going to ruin me. If that cocksucker talks, I'm gonna land in jail. I practically raised that mother fucker, and now he's gonna make me the

first president of the United States to spend the last days of his life behind bars.... Oh, I tell you, John, it only takes one prick to ruin a man in this town.... And I'm getting fucked by two bastards – Bobby and that Williams son of a bitch."

Then, in a controversial article on February 5, Johnson got a break. My uncle's leaked Air Force and State Department files were made public in an article written by the famous columnist, Drew Pearson, printed in the *Washington Post*. (Apparently, Special Assistant Secretary to the Air Force Benjamin Fridge, on his own volition, had written a special memorandum to Secretary of the Air Force Eugene Zuckert. Fridge was the one who had released confidential information from Air Force and State Department files to the famous columnist.)

On February 8, 1964, LBJ recounted to Moyers that the files had been leaked. Moyers mentioned that people had told him it was good that this "guy was finally exposed." From those records, it appeared that Don Reynolds would have been kicked out of both institutions had it not been for Joe McCarthy. LBJ commented that he couldn't understand why newspapers had been protecting a man like that.

The article wasn't a pleasant read for our family. My uncle had been lying about his West Point record (he had actually flunked out), engaging in immoral conduct and black market activities in Germany, and furnishing false information to U.S. government officials.

My uncle, taking the long view, saw the subterfuge. It was a smear. The information was probably true, but irrelevant. *"Whatever my past,"* he stated for the *Washington Post*, "this had absolutely nothing to do with the recent events involving LBJ, Bobby Baker, or Walter Jenkins."

However, that didn't stop famed reporter, Jack Anderson (who worked for Pearson) from shouting:

> The past is prologue! We have already exposed in our column the unreliability of your star witness, Don Reynolds, whose sordid record as an informant goes back to the heyday of the late Senator Joe McCarthy.
>
> We won't review all the facts that we have already published about Reynolds, except to say he has made a career of bringing false charges against those who cross him. He has made complaints to the FBI against so many people, charging that they were Communists and sex deviates, that the FBI finally investigated him in 1952. This led a Security Review Board to conclude that he was a security risk.

His confidential file declares, "A Security Review Board in the United States Air Force concluded in 1953 that Reynolds' past led to a reasonable belief that he was a security risk. This judgment was based on his habits, activities, attitudes, associations, trustworthiness, discretion, and loyalty." In June 1953, Senator Joseph McCarthy attempted to intervene in the review of Reynolds' security.

McCarthy, who had condemned others on far less evidence than the FBI had gathered against Reynolds, succeeded in saving his informant from a dishonorable discharge. Reynolds continued whispering in McCarthy's ear after the FBI would have nothing to do with him. Now this committee has resurrected Reynolds and made him a star witness against the President.

The same day that Pearson's article was released, my uncle wrote to Senator Williams, detailing a call he had previously received from Bobby Baker at the Racquet Club in Montego Bay, Jamaica. Baker had referred to the insurance policy on the Vice President and wanted to know how much of a kickback he could get on the insurance commission. My uncle said to never use that word on the telephone, and Bobby changed it to "rebate." Uncle Buck also received a call that day from Walter Jenkins, who told him to work out the arrangement (for Johnson's kickbacks) with Bobby, but to be sure it was in cash.

This served as the backdrop for our family's letters and correspondence during February of 1964.

CHAPTER SIX

Correspondence and A Senate Conclusion

A concerned citizen wrote a letter to my uncle. Wisconsin resident, Leonard Pasek, viewed my uncle as a Walter Mitty-type character, and one-man-against-the-establishment. (A view with which I largely concur.)

> February 11, 1964
> Mr. Don B. Reynolds
> 8485 Fenton
> Silver Spring, Maryland
>
> Dear Mr. Reynolds,
>
> Like most every American I have watched the Bobby Baker case very closely. I was in Washington and saw the Drew Pearson column which endeavored to damage you so unmercifully. I have seen you twice on newscasts and was particularly proud and pleased of the way you conducted yourself on Walter Cronkite's program last evening.
>
> There is no doubt in my mind that you are the key to performing a great service for our country, and I want you to know I am no different than millions of other Americans who want you to do everything you can to expose the truth in this widespread scandal. It takes a brave person to say what you did yesterday, which indicates to me you have what it takes to set this whole case right.
>
> Sincerely,
>
> Leonard E. Pasek
> 120 Green Bay Road Appleton, Wisconsin

My Aunt Jerry wrote back with emotion and clarity about what she saw as my uncle's valiant attempt to expose the corruption at the heart of The Hill, her fear of imminent danger, and the important role of Senator John Williams.

March 12, 1964

Mr. Leonard E. Pasek
120 Green Bay Road
Appleton, Wisconsin

Dear Mr. Pasek,

Thank you for your words of encouragement. During these difficult days Don and I have cherished the letters we've received from our families and friends, and it is especially gratifying to have a letter from someone we do not know, who understands the underlying complexity of this present scandal and sees the need to do something about it.

Right from the beginning, Don was determined to tell the truth about what he saw and knew was going on the Hill even if he got hurt. He felt that our country deserves better than it is getting. The risk he took is that people are so apathetic about the mess in Washington – or so stunned from the shock of Kennedy's death – they will not be moved to take any action to clean up their government.

When he was called in to see Senator Williams, Don said that he felt the investigation of Bobby Baker should include those who permitted him – or even taught him – the ways and means of using influence and power to make money. Don admitted that he had done some things wrong. Bobby had, too, but the real danger to our country lies in the circle of influence and corruption which stems from the heart of the Hill.

Senator Williams shares this point of view. He does not want to hurt any one person. He has not been vindictive, nor has he played the part of a crusader. He has systematically sought to expose the ramification of the Baker case in order to help Congressmen and Senators better conduct their own activities. His bipartisan attitude has been what has made us trust him.

As Don's wife, I've been frightened by the exposure of the ties of underworld characters to our politicians, as well as those of the entrepreneurs who have so much to gain or lose in business with the government. As his wife, I'm awfully proud of him too, Mr. Pasek, for standing up and declaring the truth and not being frightened or unduly concerned by the underhanded and slanderous attack on his character.

We have nothing to gain from this awful publicity and everything to lose – maybe even our lives – by "fighting city hall." But it has to start somewhere with someone, and if enough people like you understand the basic principles for which Don is fighting, then the effort will have been worth it.

Sincerely
Jerry Reynolds

After receiving Mr. Pasek's letter, my aunt reached out to my mom, Connie (in a letter that my mom kept all her life).

February 15, 1964

Dearest Connie,

Sunday got away without a call. There were too many things happening!

The crap is still thick and heavy around us. DP [Drew Pearson] is apparently the spokesman for LBJ now – at least his staunch defender – his tactics frighten Genevieve – guess she knows better than we do how rough the press can be. She called me again yesterday morning trying to save Don – she feels he's destroying himself. And I guess she shook me up. I've tried so hard to be Don's support – being a good listener – pointing out articles he should read, being grateful for good press stories, meeting news and TV people with him so they'll see me as a part of his life – when he felt he needed me besides him.

I've tried also to discuss "both sides," to point out negatives and positives, and I've not tried to hide the fact that I am a coward, or at least afraid of what could happen. Actually, I'm not afraid for me. I'm just as concerned as Genevieve that Don will get hurt – have the rug pulled out from under him. Politicians have a way of smiling from both sides of their faces, and none is above using a pawn in an election year. So, I am aware of dangers in this situation.

The thing that makes me so proud though Connie, is that Don is fighting for principles. He feels even if he does get hurt if he can he's going to contribute his efforts to clean up the mess here he's seen. You know he was close enough to the whirlpool to know what was going on – he pulled back in time to not get swept hopelessly into the Baker mess, but he knows so much. He's my knight on a white charger or maybe a Don Quixote. He's got a reason to live that involves more than making money – or playing house – or having fun. He's been just wonderful, he's not too tense – he's not afraid – and he's working like mad to help make this a better world for [our nephew.] Bobby.

I hope he'll understand some day.

We need your prayers and your love –
You have ours.
Jerry

There was no doubt that Senator John Williams provided tremendous support for my uncle during the scandal. Frankly, I don't think he would have survived without the Delaware Senator's help. My aunt recognized his assistance:

> March 12, 1964
>
> The Honorable John Williams
> Senate Office Building
> Washington, D.C.
>
> Dear Senator Williams,
> We received a heartwarming letter from an unknown man in Wisconsin which we want to share with you. I am enclosing a copy of my reply as a way of expressing our gratitude for the gentlemanly way you have proceeded with the Baker case.
> We deeply appreciate your guidance and many kindnesses to us.
>
> Sincerely,
> Mrs. Don. B. Reynolds

From the end of November 1963 to the end of February 1964, there were intense pressures building within our family. The President and his administration were saying one thing, but the presidential tapes, my uncle's testimony, and LBJ's actions (abusing the FBI) indicated another. There would only be more pressure points and more political drama in the days and months ahead.

***

In March 1964, the U.S. Senate officially rendered their verdict. Senator John Williams, the news media, and our family were underwhelmed with the judgment. It only recommended a pallid reform to investigate the financial activities of Senate employees. My uncle's testimony was ignored.

As Clark Mollenhoff wrote in *Despoilers of Democracy*, "What does it say when a man like Reynolds, who had a less than a clean past, comes forward and is treated in this fashion?"

Why did our nation's highly respected institution, the U.S. Senate, the most deliberative body in the world, propound such fantasy? Did the Senate have an underlying motive?

CHAPTER SEVEN

JUDGING, TRUST, AND TWO SENATE WITNESSES

MARCH 1964

> *I feel that as an American citizen, ex-service man and civil servant, my rights have been abridged and my character is at stake. It appears you have permitted a conspiracy to discredit my testimony for having known these people and embarrassing them.*
>
> – Don Reynolds, in a letter to Senator Everett Jordan, NC, March 14, 1964

One day in my not-so-distant past, I was talking with my boss, the local DeForest, Wisconsin Postmaster, regarding his work force: his city and rural letter carriers (the latter of which I was one). He told me his philosophy. "Bob," he said, "I trust my people, until they give me a reason not to."

It reminded me what our legal system is supposed to be based upon: a person is presumed innocent until proven guilty. Not everyone lives by that idea, though. Donald Reynolds offered, at least at one time, a slightly more pessimistic view of life.

Uncle Buck left the States in fear of his life and the Johnson administration. He lived in the Bahamas, in exile from 1965 to 1969 (however, he did occasionally come back to the United States during that time for testimony). I was unable to see him during one of his visits to Washington, D.C., so we communicated by phone. I expressed my regrets at not being able to see him in person. He also regretted not seeing me, but at that time, he wanted to give me some unsolicited advice. (At that age, for me, most advice was unsolicited!) "You've got a good mind, but don't let people try to contaminate it, Bob. Keep looking, Bob – *don't take anybody's word* – keep checking."

I took him to mean *guard your mind in ambiguous situations*, and, in other, more benign circumstances, *try to keep an open mind*. Just because someone has the title of doctor, or president, or senator, doesn't exempt them from review – make people, despite their professions, prove their assertions.

Uncle Buck departed this world in 1993, so sadly, I don't have the ability to "keep checking," at least not with him.

When should someone take the time to check and recheck judgments, particularly of people or institutions we hold in high esteem? Would you trust until you are given a reason not to or, would you not take anybody's word at face value? Maybe we should trust, but still verify, just to be thorough.

Would you believe the judgment of a U.S. Senate Rules Investigating Committee without checking the facts yourself? What about a doctor, a judge, the IRS? It is part of our citizenship to keep our institutions responsible.

(In 2013, The Wisconsin Court of Appeals reversed a lower court decision from a Madison judge, and found in my favor. I also won an appeal from the IRS in 2016. My attorney and I didn't take judgments at face value. We took the time to study and had the courage to press our case. Perhaps unconsciously, I had taken my uncle's advice to heart!)

But why did Don Reynolds choose to give me that advice at that specific time? I believe it had to do with two judgments of the Senate, one in July 1964, and one in March 1965. Both of those judgments released pressure and deflected attention away from the President of the United States.

No one likes to be judged. Yet judgments are necessary in a civil society, otherwise, the guilty would go free and we would descend into lawlessness. It's best if the judgment rendered is correct, or, if not, some understandable mistake or context can be offered for the misjudgment – particularly if the bad judgment doesn't have enormous implications.

In my opinion, it's lamentable that the first report of the Senate: Senate Report 1175, filed July 8, 1964, was neither complete, nor its intentions above reproach.

At this point in 1964, there was conflicting testimony from a Maryland insurance broker, a presidential aide, and the President of the United States regarding potential kickbacks. Would you believe the President as opposed to a potentially angry and obscure Maryland insurance broker who'd had a troubled past? All things equal, I know what I would naturally do: I would believe the President … unless, of course, (as my postmaster boss would say), the President gave me a reason not to.

The thirty-sixth President gave me reason not to.

The secret LBJ tapes give some background as to why my uncle, in this case, had the correct approach. (Johnson was on the phone more than any president in U.S. history. He directed that if he died suddenly, his secretary, Mildred Stegall, would ensure that the secret tape recordings of his conversations were destroyed, or, would not be released until 2023, fifty years after his death. She did *not* carry out that wish ... Then, Lady Byrd Johnson, and the president of the LBJ Library, Harry Middleton, decided to release the tapes early in 1990.

On a tape dated February 8, 1964, LBJ confers with Hubert Humphrey on the scandal. Johnson's concerned yet defiant rhetoric betrayed his hubris: "This is just between you, and me, and God, Hubert. [Senator Richard] Russell said they want to call a number of witnesses. [Senator Carl] Curtis is trying to get an amendment where any senator can call a witness, instead of the Majority ... so they can call Walter Jenkins! ... Of course, I wouldn't let Walter Jenkins go..." Humphrey responded with a muffled. "Right."

This meant bad news for people trying to get to the truth. The President of the United States was plotting to shut down the investigation by not calling a witness, and the man he picked as the Chairman of the investigation, Everett Jordan, pledged to sway the investigation.

There used to be saying about the Senate: "To get along, you have to go along." The secret presidential tapes seem to confirm that there was indeed immense pressure to make peace, to not stick out, and to not raise uncomfortable questions. Those six Democrats would need enormous courage to defy the President of the United States and their party ... courage that they apparently did not possess.

On March 13, 1964, Chairman Everett Jordan stated, "We have reached the point where the taking of further testimony in this situation would serve no legislative purpose.... This is the duty of the U.S. Senate, not that of the Democrats or of the Republicans. Throughout this investigation, I have bent over backwards to be fair and nonpartisan."

In all fairness, there were hundreds of pages of testimony, documents, four months of hard work, witnesses interviewed.... That should have been enough.... But this was the same Everett Jordan who promised LBJ, on tape, that he would stop the "fire from spreading."

On March 16, in the Congressional Record, Senator Hubert Humphrey said:

> I reject the charge that because three members of the committee ask that something be done, and six members consider sufficient work has been done to complete one phase of the responsibility of the committee, those six want a so-called whitewash. Since when have those three had a right to hold themselves up as paragons of virtue while the other six are to be held up as their antitheses?

So, this senator rejected out of hand the charge of whitewash ... but let's not forget that this was the same senator who listened to LBJ saying he would make sure a witness was not called – the witness that contradicted my uncle's testimony.

The Senate report was excellent for LBJ. It was an official imprimatur; it could stop the crises from spreading – the rolling crises that had enveloped him since October 1963. He was now the President. He had the power to control the Senate.

The Senate report fell short of full investigation for two primary reasons: Rule 19, which allowed any senator to call witnesses was not allowed, and the witnesses that the Republican minority suggested that the Democrats call were all voted down.

Clark Mollenhoff wrote:

> Despite public pressure for continuing the investigation, the Democratic members of the Senate Rules Committee were set on ending it.... The Republicans sought permission to send out their own investigator. It was denied them. They had submitted a list of more than fifteen witnesses including Jenkins, who they felt should be called. Their requests were steamrollered by power of numbers in early March."
>
> Senator Scott (R, PA) said, "It is a pity to have the investigation end in this fashion.... If we do an inadequate job or a partial job or if we quit when there is another group of witnesses to be heard – perhaps half as many – I do not think the people ever will think this investigation was other than what one newspaper characterized it – that is, a tawdry investigation – and that a stain will remain on the integrity of the Senate."
>
> In spite of repeated efforts to point out that, in fairness, under our legislative proceedings, all witnesses should be required to undergo the same procedure under the rule, and testify under oath, the committee displayed favoritism toward one witness, and it denied that treatment to another witness.

On March 12, 1964, the *Washington Star* printed:

> Those who have been trying to identify that unpleasant odor floating around the Senate side of the Capitol need go no further. It's whitewash.
>
> Apparently, the committee, or the controlling members of the committee, have had enough. They don't want to develop the whole truth for the education of the public.
>
> The excuse offered is that there are no more witnesses who might be called. This is nonsense. What about Walter Jenkins? Senator Williams, Republican of Delaware, has just given the committee an affidavit from Don B. Reynolds, a Silver Spring insurance man, which raises grave questions respecting Mr. Jenkins. Shouldn't these be explored – at least to the extent of trying to pin down the truth?
>
> Why is the committee so afraid to explore the matter?

Senator Carl Curtis said:

> The committee denied, six to three, a motion to recall Don Reynolds as a witness. His testimony had been given in executive session, not in public session; it was highly important testimony, worth reviewing in the light of testimony by others. Reynolds had been subject to repeated attacks by the committee's majority. Reynolds was excluded.

The controversy was picked up by the *Garrett County Republican* newspaper in Maryland – where my uncle maintained his farmhouse in the rural town of Oakland.

> Bobby Baker and Don Reynolds remain in the news columns and their activities remain of interest to Garrett County readers.
>
> The last time was one where the Democratic-controlled Senate Rules Committee had turned thumbs down on a return engagement for the witness who brought President Johnson's name into the Baker investigation. "Immaterial and irrelevant" was the committee's pronouncement on a new affidavit by insurance man Don B. Reynolds. Reynolds told earlier hearings that he gave Johnson a $585 stereo set while selling him two $100,000 life insurance policies....
>
> The committee which had been investigating Baker's outside business activities while he was Secretary to the Senate's Democratic Majority, voted 6 to 3 at a closed meeting against recalling Reynolds.

On April 30, 1964, the *Republican* wrote:

> Despite Democratic efforts to close the lid on the Bobby Baker investigation, the Pandora's Box continues to pop open with tales of shakedowns and high-powered arm twisting.
>
> Through it all, this fundamental point remained: Senate Rules Committee Democrats, using their 6-3 majority, had shut off the probe well before all the facts came out. One widely-concluded reason: The committee was fearful of further implicating high-placed Administration officials – including perhaps President Johnson himself.

My uncle could see the writing on the wall for his personal situation. He pleaded directly with Senator Jordan one last time:

> March 16, 1964
>
> Senator Everett Jordan
> U.S. Senate
> Washington, D.C.
>
> Dear Sir:
> This letter is written with the expressed desire that you as Senate Rules Committee Chairman clarify beyond any reasonable doubt the truthfulness of the statements I made under oath in the matter pertaining to the purchase of TV time arranged by Walter Jenkins, and the question of rebate requested by Mr. Jenkins and Bobby Baker, as furnished in my supplemental affidavits.
>
> I should like to point out that there is no double standard under our system of democracy as expressed in the Constitution where one man, who is an ordinary citizen, takes an oath and answers all questions, and another man, because of his politically appointed position, merely submits an affidavit attached to the statements of two investigators.
>
> I know that my statements are completely true and I respectfully request that you either call Mr. Jenkins before your committee and question him under oath, or that you issue a categorical statement to me, which shall be published, that all of my sworn testimony regarding the negotiations with Walter Jenkins for the purchase of TV time on station KTCB is true and correct, and that the supplemental affidavit concerning further attempts to obtain rebate on the insurance conversion is true and correct.
>
> I feel that as an American citizen, an ex-serviceman, and civil servant, my character is at stake and that my rights have been

abridged. It appears that you have permitted a conspiracy to discredit my testimony for having known these people and certain facts embarrassing to them.

I appeal to you, not in your position as a politician, but as an American with a high sense of responsibility, to remove the clouds of doubt that will persist because of the conflict in testimony. This communication is directed to you out of no political motivation – nor for any other purpose than to urge that justice and right rule over power politics.

Please give me an answer at your earliest possible convenience.

Sincerely yours,
Don B. Reynolds

I noticed that my uncle's plea to Senator Jordan bore a striking resemblance to the letter that Elliot Maraniss wrote to the Senate regarding his situation in 1953 during the Red Scare:

> I was taught as a child and in school that the highest responsibility of citizenship is to defend the principles of the U.S. Constitution and to do my part in securing for the American people the blessings of peace, economic well-being, and freedom....
>
> And for doing that – and nothing more – I have been summarily discharged from my job. I have been blacklisted in the newspaper business after 12 years in which my competency and objectivity have never once been questioned.
>
> I must sell my home, uproot my family, and upset the tranquility and security of my three small children in the happy, formative years of their childhood.
>
> But I would rather have my children miss a meal or two now than have them grow up in the gruesome, fear-ridden future for America projected by the members of the House Committee on Un-American Activities....
>
> This committee reflects no credit on American institutions or ideas....
>
> I am confident that the people of Detroit will reject this committee's effort to subvert the U.S. Constitution."[16]

My uncle's travails were soon to parallel what happened to Maraniss. It was a story of same church, different pew: two Senate witnesses and two Senate judgments – judgments that, although at different times and circumstances, muddied the integrity of the Senate.

16   Maraniss, David, *A Good American Family: The Red Scare and My Father*, Simon & Schuster 2019.

On July 27, both Senator Curtis and Senator Williams reached out to Senator Jordan regarding the committee's research, and lamented that Matt McCloskey, the man responsible for construction of the DC stadium, was not called in the Senate report. Senator Curtis said, "The facts are not all available. Mr. McCloskey was never called." To which Senator Williams agreed:

> I concur in what the Senator from Nebraska stated. Mr. McCloskey should have been called.... But what the committee does not have and which the committee should have and which I hope it will still try obtain is a copy of Mr. McCloskey's check to Mr. Reynolds as payment for this stadium insurance. I think it would be very important to have that information.

Instead of following up on Williams' lead, Senator Jordan said:

> I think the record shows what the amount is. The report shows what he paid for the performance bond, but I shall not argue the point.

Did Senator Jordan not argue the point because he didn't get the point – or was he just "stopping the fire"? The cost of the bond was a certain amount, but that didn't necessarily mean that was the amount that Mr. McCloskey paid to my uncle, as Senator Williams added:

> While it may be merely routine, I should like to see the $73,631.28 check to see if that is exactly what was paid. I would suggest that even now the committee should obtain a copy of that check. It may be interesting.

It was one last attempt to shake the Senate into action ... the Senate then took a sleeping pill and went to bed.

The Senate had completely disregarded my uncle's testimony: there was nothing of import, nothing to see – Reynolds' testimony was immaterial and irrelevant. They even ignored Senator Williams' plea to investigate the check in August. To the Senate, everything was now in the rear-view mirror, but there was still more to come. Senator Williams waited because he needed proof of the check amount.... A photostatic copy of that check was hand delivered to him at his office in the middle of the night.

My uncle bragged to the news media in August 1964, "Wait until they get the surprise after the convention." (It was an election year.) The disputed check from builder Matt McCloskey to Don Reynolds would create consequences for the Senate, but unbeknownst to Uncle Buck, first there would be an unwelcome and scorching surprise for him.

CHAPTER EIGHT

A Mysterious Fire, The Senate Shocker, LBJ's Fourth Crisis, and A Secreted Star

At 6:00 PM I received a call from Don Reynolds. He was in Arizona incognito and admitted he was considering going to a country for an asylum. He said he was in fear of his life and his wife was on the verge of a complete breakdown.
— The John Williams Papers, University of Delaware, Newark

Oakland, Maryland is a picturesque town in Garrett County in the western mountains of Maryland, three hours away from the political hustle and bustle of the nation's capital.

Not far from West Virginia, it is one of the coldest places in Maryland, and is ideally suited for wintertime recreational activities. It is where my Aunt Jerry and Uncle Buck escaped to less stressful summer vacations. My uncle and Bobby Baker were well known in the county for their earlier interest in developing a ski lodge in the nearby mountains. However, it was other entrepreneurs that eventually developed the famous Wisp Ski Resort, the popular downhill ski destination that is nestled near the town today.

Oakland is where I enjoyed my summers with my aunt and uncle from 1959 to 1964. Exploring the woods near their farmhouse, swimming, and boating with them on Deep Creek Lake remain some of the most enjoyable memories from my youth.

***

I traveled back to Oakland on my East Coast trip in the summer of 2020. I spent a few hours at Deep Creek Lake beach taking in the beautiful views and the memories of long ago, but I hadn't travelled to the town just to reminisce. I stopped at the Garrett County Library and asked Amy, the research librarian, to help a friend of the family and me solve a mystery that had frustrated both of us for years.

"We don't have a name index for *The Garrett County Republican*. You'll have to go through the microfilm collection for that year," Amy said.

An hour of research yielded some clues from the *Garrett County Republican*, September 3, 1964:

> The remodeled farm home of Don B. Reynolds, Silver Spring insurance man and real estate promoter in this county, was completely destroyed by fire last Thursday night about 10 o'clock. The home was located north of Gnegy Church, just off U.S. route 219. ["Last Thursday" was August 27, 1964.]
>
> Mr. Reynolds had been at his home earlier in the day, but at the time of the fire, there was no one at home. The Oakland firemen were called but the flames had enveloped the house completely before the truck made the twelve-mile run to the property. Mr. Reynolds had spent several thousand dollars in remodeling the building last year. The loss was partially covered by insurance.

As soon as I had the location, I headed out from the library on Maryland route 219. I turned off at Gnegy Church Road, but I became confused because nothing looked familiar. A woman from a mobile home came out, saw my Wisconsin plate, and asked if she could help. "Oh, you're looking for Roth-Reynolds Road," she said, "that's a quarter mile north of here, off Hwy 219, you're almost there."

Once on the right road, I was fortunate enough to meet one of the residents, Dan Beckman, who had lived at that location for many years. With Dan, I walked along the road that led to the farmhouse, but a gate blocked us from actually getting on the property.

I was struck by the appearance of the road. It seemed like it was just as rural and isolated as it had been when I last visited over fifty-five years prior. Not surprisingly, Oakland's population hadn't grown much since the 1950s.

Through Dan's referral, I called Stuart Thayer (another friend who knew my uncle). He told me about the famous people who had visited my uncle's farmhouse, including the actor, Richard Boone, from the popular TV show *Have Gun, Will Travel*. "Did your uncle tell you about the time he was hiding at the Pease farm with shotguns?" asked Stuart. (He had not!)

Neither Dan nor Stuart mentioned anything about the farmhouse fire, but their nondisclosure, together with Stuart's startling shotgun question, seemed to indicate that there were a number of residents in the county who knew more about an untold past.

After the fateful fire, my uncle remarked that it had happened under "suspicious circumstances." He told a friend of the family a story, which in turn was shared with me almost sixty years later. A neighbor (perhaps Dan Beckman's father) had seen a car that he didn't recognize drive down Roth-Reynolds road a couple of hours before the farmhouse blaze sprung up. "Bob, if that's true," the friend said to me, "there are two conclusions: either someone was very lost, or someone had a very specific reason to be driving down that isolated, dead-end road."

Had the fire been a last-ditch effort to intimidate Don Reynolds before his surprise for the Senate Democrats became public?

A few years before she died, my mom confirmed to me that investigators could not determine the cause of the fire. It was a frustrating piece of history for everyone in our family. His sister, Mary Lou, later remarked to me, "I bet he wishes today he had that money that literally all went up in smoke."

The mystery in Oakland remained.

***

On September 1, 1964, Senator Williams announced the shock to the Senate that my uncle had known was coming. It blindsided the Senate Democrats. The *Congressional Record* from September 1, 1964 stated:

> Mr. President, today I call the attention of the Senate to some new evidence which has been developed in the Bobby Baker case.
>
> This new evidence involves an additional kickback of over $35,000 which was made by Mr. Matthew McCloskey on the Washington stadium contract.
>
> Of this extra kickback $25,000 was scheduled through Bobby Baker for the 1960 Democratic campaign fund. The rest represents payments to the individuals handling this transaction. In this conspiracy to channel the additional $35,000 payoff into Washington several laws were violated.
>
> This new evidence involves an additional kickback of over $35,000 which was made by Mr. Mathew McCloskey on the Washington stadium contract.
>
> There are many who could not understand why the Democratic membership of the Senate Rules Committee were so determined not to call certain witnesses to testify in the Bobby Baker investigation.
>
> Two of these key witnesses whom the Rules Committee, by a vote of 6 to 3, refused to allow to testify in a public session were Mr. Don B. Reynolds and Mr. Matthew H. McCloskey, Jr.

This detailed the first felony (wrapped up in a conspiracy) that my uncle committed. There were more to come. My uncle was known as the Star Witness of this scandal. Such a title showed the importance of his testimony, and the unwillingness of certain senators to face the truth (it also showed their purposeful intent to hide the truth!) This is why both Senator Williams and Senator Curtis would later say there was a "diabolical" scheme of certain senators to conceal the facts (not a great way to increase collegiality among your fellow senators!). Then again, John Williams was never one to go along to get along.

Senator Williams wrote in his papers:

> Mr. Reynolds did testify in executive session, but he was refused an opportunity to testify in public session even though he requested such an opportunity, and even though the Minority membership of the Rules Committee kept insisting that his testimony would be very important.
>
> Perhaps after today's report it can be more readily understood why someone in the high command ordered these hearings closed.

In his book *It Didn't Start with Watergate*, Victor Lasky mentioned that at this point in time, no one wanted to point a finger at a president. I believe this is why Johnson was not specifically named and implicated. If Senator Jordan personally shut the hearings down, he was taking his orders from 1600 Pennsylvania Avenue.

When Senator Williams concluded his speech on the Senate floor, he said:

> The Johnson administration in Atlantic City last week said that it believed in integrity in government. Here is a chance to demonstrate whether they mean it.
>
> The choice lies between full disclosure or political whitewash, and the United States Senate and the Johnson Administration will be judged by their decision.

The senator had a combination of persistence, investigative skill, and honesty. These three qualities were a serious combination for people like Lyndon Johnson and Bobby Baker.

(Growing up on a farm, Williams never graduated from high school, but couldn't a man, blessed with forthrightness, persistence, and the full use of his mind, be the equal of other men who'd had an earlier start?) Already known in *Time* by the phrase: "He found the rascals out" (being used in regards to his work rooting out IRS corruption), Williams was the man with whom my uncle found solace and shelter during the scandal, and he was probably the only man who could have orchestrated the end of Bobby Baker's and LBJ's careers.

***

Williams was up for reelection; Johnson knew he was in for a fight. While travelling to Dover, Delaware, LBJ exclaimed, "Give me men I can work with!" He must have believed his time was well spent to defeat the "son of a bitching Williams"; otherwise, why would he have spent his time in a state with only three electoral votes? The Democratic challenger Edwin Carvel said, "Delaware needs a statesman, not a policeman." Delaware's electors went Democratic, but the citizens knew better – they voted independently, sending Williams back for his third, six-year term.

***

The turn of events in September 1964 was remarkable: one man – Don Buck Reynolds, with the help of Senator Williams – had forced the Senate to reopen the Bobby Baker investigation. But just when our family thought we could relax, we discovered that there was yet more turbulence ahead.

In late September 1964, LBJ got his political rifle ready. In *All the Way with LBJ: The 1964 Presidential Election* (which explores the contents of LBJ's presidential recordings), said LBJ was preparing to "fight dirty" with Don Reynolds:

> I think it's a question of who's going to survive … whether McCloskey survives. I think if McCloskey takes a position that he did make a political contribution, why, he's had it.
>
> And I think it's a question of whether the party's had it or not, because he has been the National Financial Chairman of the Democratic Party in the United States. I think that's number one. I think, number two, he is the Democratic Party in Pennsylvania, which is a very key state, and this gets back into an Insull Deal, or a Teapot Dome Deal in the state of Pennsylvania.
>
> And Scranton will be getting into it, and they'll be destroying the Democratic Party there.
>
> Now, it's a question of who's going to destroy who.
>
> My judgment is, that Bobby has got some bad marks on him, and so has McCloskey.
>
> But the two of them can probably show this fellow doesn't have much character. And they can go back and make them subpoena the records and see what kind of guy he is. What is his purpose in doing

this, what is his motive? Is he just a good clean citizen, or is he a guy that's been abducting little thirteen-year-old girls? And that's what they're tied up with.

Politics consumed LBJ; he had to win. Don Reynolds put his standing and power at risk; LBJ could order just a smear campaign – or the threatened President could go further.

This was another crisis, the fourth that LBJ had to deal with. The first was the Baker scandal, hitting while LBJ was in Copenhagen; the second devastating blow was my uncle's testimony on November 22, 1963; the third, when LBJ ran from the press conference on January 27, 1964 after being asked about the stereo given by my uncle; and now, Senator Williams' surprise to the Senate continued the onslaught of shockwaves that battered LBJ's defenses.... The Senate report, engineered by Landslide Lyndon in 1964, hadn't done the trick after all.

***

My uncle regretted that he had allowed himself to be the intermediary, channeling illegal campaign contributions to the 1960 Democratic campaign for Johnson. Baker had initiated those dealings, but apparently, my uncle didn't have the fortitude or wisdom to walk away. He admitted he was the "bagman" – the funnel by which illegal funds were transferred.

Considering I was twelve years old at the time, my parents decided to store news articles in a safe place, left to posterity. My mom saved two articles from the major media of the day; I discovered them after she had passed away. *US News and World Report,* December 13, 1964 stated, "Testimony of Don B. Reynolds, an insurance broker and self-described 'bagman' in dealings which according to Mr. Reynolds, Bobby Baker masterminded, touched off the latest explosions." The December 14, 1964 issue of *Newsweek* detailed, "Burly Maryland insurance man Don B. Reynolds came on as a key informant – the self-styled 'bagman' in the alleged kickback by McCloskey – but was treated like a hostile witness by Committee Counsel Lennox P. McLendon."

That word was mentioned in our family many times during the scandal. My mom would describe everything that my uncle did with McCloskey with that one word: bagman. Then, with deep sadness, she would turn her head away. If the threats to LBJ didn't go away, the stress on our family didn't go away either.

One night, long before the sun was up, I was awakened by my mom and dad having a discussion in hushed tones in the bedroom across from mine. Then, the still air was shattered as my mom yelled, "Well, he's my brother!" The strain was getting to everyone: Uncle Buck and his wife; my Aunt Mary Lou, frightened for her brother; my mom and dad, fighting in the wee hours of the morning. I wondered if it would ever come to an end.

"What is one thing whose supply always exceeds the demand: Trouble." This answer to an economics professor's question seemed to typify the crux of the problem facing our family in October 1964. My uncle had returned to Oakland after the farmhouse fire. It seemed like he was trying to flee the trouble in D.C., but he couldn't quite escape it. Even in such a small town, Uncle Buck was embroiled in more Sturm und Drang. He sought peace and quiet, but he also seemed to be itching for a fight – even when cornered by the Internal Revenue Service.

IRS Special Agent Donald R. Connelly told the Senate Rules Committee that Don B. Reynolds said he would have to be given proof that the IRS was investigating the income tax return of President Johnson and Walter Jenkins (a top V.P. assistant), before he would surrender some of his own tax records for examination. Connelly said Reynolds first made the demand at a chance meeting on a street in Oakland, and repeated it the next day (October 15, 1964) at a conference in the office of Attorney Stephen Pagenhardt, the Oakland lawyer representing Reynolds' insurance firm.[17]

Just one day before (October 14), Walter Jenkins had resigned as President Johnson's aide after the story of his October 7 arrest was released in the press (despite the immense pressure Johnson applied to have the story buried). Jenkins had been apprehended in a YMCA men's room, in Washington D.C, on a morals charge. (The incident led to one of the slogans for Republican Nominee Barry Goldwater, "All the way with LBJ, but don't go near the YMCA." Bill Moyers then filled the position of LBJ's loyal aide that Jenkins had left vacant.

Goldwater thought the Baker affairs ran straight into the White House. Upon hearing about Jenkins' sexual orientation, Goldwater stated, "What a way to win an election. Communists and cocksuckers." It was not at all charitable, but the main issue wasn't sexual preference, it was the conflicting testimony between Jenkins and my uncle.

LBJ was faced with multiple entangled problems: Williams was still in the Senate, my uncle was a loose cannon threatening to derail his career, Bobby Baker was being investigated (if Baker talked, LBJ would be in trouble), and now, LBJ had lost his long-standing trusted aide.

---

17   Rada, James, Cumberland Times, February 3, 2020.

***

My uncle had done some heavy political lifting. New revelations forced the Senate to reopen the investigation, and accordingly, a subpoena was issued for Uncle Buck to appear before the Rules Committee on December 1, 1964. But after bragging about the big surprise, it seemed as if my uncle had second thoughts. Soon, the question on everyone's lips was, "Where is the star witness, Don Buck Reynolds?"

On November 6, Senator Williams addressed that very question in his personal papers.

> Earlier today I talked to Clark Mollenhoff and he was concerned that Mr. Reynolds may be planning to leave the country rather than to testify. He was not sure whether this was as the result of fear of his life or for his family or whether someone had reached him.
>
> Likewise, I talked today with Mr. Hoft and he too had the impression that Mr. Reynolds was being scared off or had decided not to testify, and Mr. Hoft's understanding was that Mr. Reynolds was in Europe. Clark did not know where he was.

In another entry, he wrote:

> At 6:00 PM tonight I received a call from Don Reynolds. He said he was in Arizona incognito, and he admitted that he was considering going to a country for an asylum. He said he was in fear of his life and his wife was on the verge of a complete breakdown. The Justice Department had harassed them to the point of destruction. He had been advised that Baker as the result of the elections had said that he was in the clear now and they were going to get Reynolds, discredit him, and put him behind bars, and that they would get John Williams.

Then, in a letter, the Senator gave some encouragement:

> I assured Mr. Reynolds that had I not been reelected they may have gotten away with it, but since I was reelected and now had 6 years they could not possibly get away with it, and by all means he should make himself available to the Committee, call their bluff and make them present Mr. McCloskey, and Mr. Baker under oath for testimony, and I promised that I would stand by him regardless to make sure that he would not be used as a goat, leaving the others to go free.
>
> I had been undecided earlier after hearing of Mr. Reynolds' disappearance as to whether he had been scared off or bought off. After talking to him on the telephone I was inclined to think he was scared. His home had been burned a few months ago under

rather strange circumstances, and the Departments were having someone contact all of his clients and insurance companies and they too were being harassed to the point where they were going to be forced from doing any business with him.

(My uncle never told me any of what had gone on behind the scenes. Perhaps, like my father's time in the Army Air Corp, and David Maraniss' father with the Red Scare, Uncle Buck wished those events to remain firmly in the past.)

My mom returned home one night and nervously exclaimed, "Uncle Buck has gotten a subpoena!" Either a process server had found my uncle, or he had made himself available.

Events were moving rapidly toward another crisis climax for LBJ. The first Senate report was old news. Would this new investigation prove delayed justice, or justice denied to my uncle? The testimony and second Senate report would either remove or cement the stain of the first one.

By this time, a full year had passed since LBJ had assumed the presidency, but it was still anyone's guess who would win the political showdown scheduled for December 1, 1964. LBJ had the Senate in his hands, but my uncle had Senator Williams and Senator Curtis, and *more importantly, he had the truth.*

U. S. News & World Report

THE BAKER CASE AGAIN—
A BAGFUL OF NEW CHARGES

Suddenly, the Bobby Baker case has come to life again.

From a "bagman" comes a charge of a political "kickback." Reports of secret testimony about corruption and party girls create shock waves. Officials wonder nervously where it's leading.

Like an unpredictable volcano, the strange case of Bobby Baker is erupting again.

New charges of corruption in high places of Government are being bared.

Hints are dropped of real shockers still kept secret—such as reports of the use of call girls to influence official decisions, intrigue involving a German beauty with a possible East German Communist background, and allegation of a $100,000 payoff in the award of a controversial aircraft contract.

The new developments burst when the Senate Rules Committee, early this month, resumed its inquiry into the affairs of Robert G. (Bobby) Baker, former secretary to the Senate's Democratic majority, who quit under fire in 1963.

Mr. Baker, now 36, rose to riches on a salary that never exceeded $19,600 a year. He was chosen as Secretary for the Majority in 1955, when Lyndon B. Johnson became Senate Majority Leader.

—USN&WR Photo
BOBBY BAKER—in the spotlight again, but still not talking much

Testimony of Don B. Reynolds, an insurance broker and self-described "bagman" in dealings which, according to Mr. Reynolds, Bobby Baker masterminded, touched off the latest explosions.

Testifying on December 1, Mr. Reynolds told the Committee that Mr. Baker had arranged for a $35,000 "kickback" on the 19.8-million-dollar District of Columbia Stadium contract.

Mr. Reynolds testified that $25,000 of the alleged "kickback" from the stadium builder, Matthew H. McCloskey, was handed over to Mr. Baker, who said it would go to the 1960 Democratic campaign fund. For acting as "bagman," Mr. Reynolds got $10,000, he said.

Contractor's denial. Mr. McCloskey, a Philadelphia contractor, former treasurer of the Democratic National Committee and the late President Kennedy's Ambassador to Ireland, vehemently denied that he connived with Mr. Baker and Mr. Reynolds to fatten Democratic coffers by illegal means.

Mr. McCloskey admitted that his firm overpaid Mr. Reynolds $35,000 for insurance on the stadium job. He insisted, however, that this resulted only because "someone in our place goofed."

The Philadelphian said he did business with Mr. Reynolds at the request of Mr. Baker after the Senate employe said he had an interest in the Reynolds insurance firm.

Called as a witness, Mr. Baker refused to talk. He pointed out that a federal grand jury is investigating his activities, then cited the Fifth Amendment and others 45 times in declining to answer the Committee's questions.

A newspaper's report. Meanwhile, secret aspects of the Baker case were starting to sizzle.

"The Washington Evening Star" on December 2 said this: "Investigators of Bobby Baker have been staggered by a mass of new allegations about kickbacks from defense contracts, involvement of Senators with call girls and other corruption in Washington.

"They also have received new reports about the deported German beauty Ellen Rometsch and about former presidential aide Walter Jenkins. The allegations are embodied in secret testimony given to the Senate Rules Committee under oath yesterday by Don B. Reynolds, once an intimate associate of Baker.

"If substantiated, they would dwarf any of the scandals which have emerged from the investigation of the former secretary to the Senate majority.

"Reaction of Senators who heard the charges was described as ranging from incredulity to horror.

"Extreme efforts are being made to prevent leakage of the testimony Reynolds offered behind closed doors.

"Even Republicans, who seldom ignore an opportunity to push the Baker *(continued on next page)*

—USN&WR Photo
DON REYNOLDS—a lot to say, but much of it as secret testimony

—Wide World Photo
MATTHEW McCLOSKEY—words to explain overpayment of $35,000

U. S. NEWS & WORLD REPORT, Dec. 14, 1964

My Uncle Buck was all over the news. It was an uneasy time.

60

CHAPTER NINE

SENATE TESTIMONY & A SENATE SHAM

DECEMBER 1964-MARCH 1965

I never met him. He's a bum that's got us involved. I don't have a thing in the world to hide ... I don't want history to say these things. I don't want to be a Harding!"
– LBJ, March 4, 1965, to Attorney General Nicholas Katzenbach regarding my uncle and his allegations.

On December 1, 1964, the telephone rang in our new home in Munster. It was our former landlord, Earl Smith. "Bobby," he implored me, "Turn on the TV; your uncle is on CBS!" I ran to switch the TV to the right channel and there he was: my Uncle Buck, a microphone right in front of him, testifying in public session before the Senate Rules Committee.

It was another wake-up call, the kind my family had been getting more and more of: the repeated FBI visits to our home, the farmhouse fire in Maryland, the *Chicago Tribune* front page articles ... They were all reminders that, try as hard as we might, there was no way we could stop the Baker scandal from crashing into our lives. My uncle was becoming almost as controversial a figure as the man for whom the scandal was named!

Few people in our neighborhood knew what was going on, but one day, it did reach our neighbors across the street. After we had left for summer vacation, the FBI showed up at our empty home. Upon finding our house vacant, they went over to the Buzkowski family to ask, "Where are the Nelsons?" Later, my mother gave me the feeling that the Buzkowski's opinion of us changed after that encounter.

One night, a classmate of mine named Brad watched the *CBS Evening News*. Roger Mudd had reported a short story on my uncle, saying he had knocked a UPI reporter to the ground. (One of the women in my family remarked to him, "Why did you do that, Buck?" He replied, "He got too close to me, nose to nose; I'd had it.") Although Brad and his mother mentioned the incident to me, they were discreet. I couldn't have been more thankful that news of the episode didn't spread to the rest of my classmates in Munster.

***

The testimony was acrimonious and contentious from the very beginning. It involved direct conflict between not only my uncle and the Committee, but also conflict between the committee members themselves. Newsweek concluded, "Few protagonists escaped insults and jibes as the Senate Rules Committee resumed its Bobby Baker hearings." Above this caption, four men were featured: Senator John Williams, Chief Counsel Major McLendon, Philadelphia builder Matt McCloskey, and Don Reynolds.

The main issue seemed to be disclosure. Uncle Buck wasn't totally forthright. While being honest, he did not disclose material facts. It was a version of "If they don't ask, then don't tell."

Senator Williams wanted to make sure that the invoice from my uncle matched up with the actual premium cost that should have been paid by McCloskey. Unfortunately, my uncle didn't keep a copy of the invoice he sent to McCloskey, and he didn't have the check (he had cashed it long ago). McCloskey had the original invoice and probably a copy of the check. Bobby Baker had a copy of the invoice, but not the check. Baker took the Fifth Amendment anyway and would not resolve the issue. The result was political fireworks.

After battling with the Senate Majority members of the Rules Committee, I believe Senator Williams and Senator Curtis would have heartily agreed that when you are up to your neck in alligators, it's hard to remember that your initial objective was to drain the swamp.

Uncle Buck testified before the Senate Rules Committee in a closed-door session before the public hearing occurred. The small number of committee members listened to his testimony to determine the facts. They would decide if the investigation would proceed or not.

Uncle Buck was already frustrated by his initial testimony, from over a year before, being completely steamrolled and disregarded. Despite the high price he had already paid through smear campaigns and personal losses, he was determined to be heard; he was determined to make a difference. Uncle Buck was tenacious, as was Senator Williams, and the push to see things through to the bitter end kept him fighting.

Senate Testimony and A Senate Sham

***

Before the Committee, Uncle Buck stated clearly and somewhat obstinately, "I heard, 'You had better keep quiet about this because I am talking to Senator Jordan in the evening, and I see everything that transfers.'"

"Who said that?" shot back Senator Jordan.

"Bobby Baker, sir."

"He said he talked to me?" Jordan did his best to sound incredulous.

Uncle Buck narrowed his eyes at Jordan and, in an impressively even tone said, "Yes, sir."

Jordan exploded with indignation, "That is a complete lie!"

Uncle Buck continued, bolstered by Jordan's loss of composure, "But by the same token he called me, and he told me that I had better keep quiet about it because they already had gotten wind of it on the committee, and if they weren't careful that he and Matt [McCloskey] were going to get together and hang me."

Who was to be believed, Bobby Baker, or Don Reynolds? Considering Senator Jordan was solely focused on trying to staunch flames before they became a conflagration, even he was not trustworthy.

Chief Investigator Major McLendon then asked my uncle why he didn't disclose the $35,000 overcharge, since he had made a good amount on the transaction. In turn, Uncle Buck was brazenly maieutic and asked McLendon directly if he, himself, would have disclosed that information. McLendon replied, "Sure, I would if I was testifying to a transaction that I participated in and made $20,000 in cash out of, and you would too."

The $20,000 consisted of two parts. The first $10,000 was a commission, legitimate for the transaction. The second $10,000 was unlawful – a bagman's fee for funneling illegal contributions to the 1960 Johnson campaign. ($20,000 then would be $140,000 today.)

McLendon continued to push, "Why did you not disclose that to the Committee?"

Uncle Buck, ever matter-of-fact and rebellious, responded "From the moment I came down to you with the information I had and the information you were trying to protect others from, sir, I felt that no matter what I did would be misconstrued."

That inflamed McLendon. "You were passing judgment on the Committee?"

"Yes, sir." Uncle Buck did not back down.

Resigned to the fact that Don Buck Reynolds would not be intimidated or belittled, McLendon steeled his resolve, "Well, what other reason can you give for not disclosing this fact?"

Uncle Buck responded, overtaking his opponent in the tête-à-tête, "The way you asked me would make me, if I were on the field of battle, to destroy you.... If you had approached me objectively without trying to insulate certain people that I had information on that may do damage and by not calling them down as witnesses, I would not have objected, sir."

Uncle Buck had attended West Point and served fifteen years in the Air Force. His time imprinted on him a "them vs. me" mentality when cornered. His combative response to McLendon essentially boiled down to: fool me once, shame on you, fool me twice, shame on me. He was also referring to the Committee's refusal to call on Walter Jenkins, which rankled my uncle no end.

McLendon refused to yield. "Mr. Reynolds, you have had eight, nine, ten opportunities with this Committee: the affidavit you made with the IRS, the interview you had with the staff of this committee, your communications to Senator Williams ... you had ten opportunities to disclose this $109,000 before you ever did it – ten times, and the only reason you give now, is because you didn't like the way the Committee was acting."

And Uncle Buck responded in kind, "Sir, it is not that I approve or disapprove. But when you are trained as a battlefield soldier, you don't like to get shoved around and other people protected who have participated."

Don Reynolds was referring to being "shoved around" by FBI Agent Ellis Meehan. My uncle recounted:

> When he threw the book down on the floor and told me I did *not* talk with Walter Jenkins about the TV advertising time, I had talked to Bobby Baker. I knew it was a falsehood and I was not going to be intimidated, sir.
>
> I had hoped that the Senate Rules Committee would have provided this cooperation and assistance. However, after my official interview with Major McLendon and the ex-FBI agent who tried to intimidate me in his questions, I decided otherwise. For example, when he asked me who discussed the purchase of television advertising space with me, and I stated that Walter Jenkins and Walter Jenkins alone had, he, the interrogator, thereupon threw a book on the floor and in a boisterous manner, informed me that I did not discuss this with Walter Jenkins, that I had discussed it with Bobby Baker.
>
> At this point I became somewhat reluctant to discuss openly anything further, knowing that his attitude was more toward defending certain people than toward ascertaining the real facts of the

case. At two subsequent appearances before the Rules Committee, I soon learned that the majority of that committee was more interested in discrediting me as a person and as a witness than it was in developing the actual facts of the case.

Is it dishonest to withhold information, especially key information and material information, from an investigating committee – information that would, in fact, exonerate you, but you feel is not the right time nor in the right hands to give?

Defense Secretary Bob McNamara had at one time, accused my uncle of being "irascible," but if you've ever experienced this kind of treatment from U.S. government officials, you might understand why my uncle, never one for understatement, said to Senator Williams, "I might as well be in Nazi Germany. They are out to get me, and they are using every government agency and every dirty trick in the book to wreck my business.... I was no angel, and I expected to be investigated, but I didn't think I would be harassed to the point that my business would be wrecked and my wife would become ill."[18]

It appeared that the FBI strategy was to shield Lyndon Johnson. If they could portray the transaction as only involving Reynolds and Baker, then it didn't extend to Texas. Simple, but effective!

Don Reynolds reacted as he did because he refused to be manipulated or browbeaten; he was already the low man on the totem pole. He had risen to America's premier military institution yet had flunked out; he had written a letter to Committee Chairman Senator Jordan but had been ignored; and, just when he wanted to break free from his past, to come clean, he was kicked around by officials of the U.S. government. He was indeed the odd man out in the transaction itself, and now before the Committee as well. His patience was running incredibly low.

(I also believe that deep down, he harbored an inferiority complex. Both Baker and my uncle hailed from the Palmetto State. Bobby, he said, came from the South Carolina hill country, whereas he came from "the poor swamplands.")

First, there was conflict between my uncle and the Committee, and then there were sparks between the Committee members themselves. Senator Williams had the floor. "I am sorry the Committee did not take that seriously enough to get Mr. McCloskey to testify."

McLendon interjected, "Well, you didn't, either."

To which Williams responed, "No."

---

18 Mollenhoff, Clark, *Despoiler of Democracy*, Doubleday & Company, Inc., 1965, page 378.

And McLendon continued. "You took Reynolds' word for it. So did we."

Senator Curtis then spoke up, "Oh, no. Listen, the Minority made a request after request that Mr. McCloskey be called, and that is in the record."

McLendon snapped back, "You are absolutely, unalterably untrue in that statement."

To which Senator Curtis responded, astounded, "This is the first time in my life that an employee of a Senate committee in a public hearing has accused a senator of an untruth."

McLendon said later that if Williams had personally called him, and mentioned this problem, he would have followed up; however, just the repeated pleas of the Minority members were apparently not enough. Thankfully, though, those requests were put in the Congressional Record and are still there for us today.

McLendon's above comment prompted Williams to walk out of the hearing.

Then, the moment of truth arrived: Curtis asked McCloskey the forbidden question. (At this point, my father – who had assisted with briefings for Allied bombers before they took off to Germany – could readily say what all bomber crews experienced: you get the toughest flak when you're directly over the target.) Curtis was directly over the target when he asked McCloskey to square his story with my uncle's. The flak exploded; Money-Man McCloskey (as my mother referred to him, with not a small amount of derision) went ballistic. He roared, "I don't care what Reynolds testified. He hasn't told the truth here once."

Curtis tried to respond, "Now, Mr. McCloskey. Do you want the committee …"

McCloskey cut him off, "Now, Mr. McCloskey *your grandmother!* That's it!"[7]

McCloskey said the $35,000 discrepancy was just a "goof." William Stewart, the controller who took the blame, later took the stand and said it could be reconciled as "general liability insurance" added to the cost of the performance bond. Under later cross examination by Senator Curtis, an employee in McCloskey's company admitted it had been coded "RFK, performance bond," not "general liability." It took an outside investigation, and four years, to uncover the company's internal error.

According to Bobby Baker, if there had been an overpayment, the money was never recovered, and *he admitted that my uncle "told the truth" about the stadium transaction.*

During the hearing, Senator Curtis asked my uncle, "Did you regard that $25,000 as a payment out of your insurance profits to Baker?"

Uncle Buck responded, "No sir."

It was not income; it was a slush fund overpayment that went directly back to Bobby Baker, in cash.

At one point, during the Senate testimony, my uncle waved a Bible on TV in front of the Committee and recited from the New Testament, "And ye shall know the truth, and the truth shall make you free." -John 8:32

I found it curious that he would lecture the Senate on religious matters. Uncle Buck didn't attend church and often didn't even seem comfortable around people of faith. I don't remember ever attending any religious services when I visited him and Aunt Jerry in Oakland or Silver Spring. He had grown up next door to the Lamar Methodist Church, and he had a close relationship with his religiously oriented sister: so perhaps now, he was having deep-rooted pangs of conscience.

It reminded me of the 2003 movie *Bonhoeffer: Agent of Grace*. Dietrich Bonhoeffer, involved in the 1944 assassination attempt on Hitler, had been brought in for questioning by the Nazis. The Nazi inquisitor thought it strange, since he was trying to seek the truth. And Bonhoeffer – a minister was trying hard to avoid it.

I still find it strange that a man with a past like Uncle Buck's should be trying so hard to get to the truth, and the Senate – which had the task of finding the truth – should be trying so hard to resist it, either through silence or falsehoods.

It's one of those bizarre contradictions in life, the ones we try hard to understand, but if we really admit it, we find hard to accept. One would not ordinarily think the Senate was engaging in subterfuge, as one would not normally think their own relative was deliberately trying to derail a Senate hearing.

***

An FBI report – which was, in fact, not produced by the FBI, but by the DOJ – in response to separate charges my uncle had made (it did not refer to the issue of Matt McCloskey) was viewed by the *NY Times* as an "extraordinary" attempt to shut the hearings down.

***

The worldview of Lyndon Johnson and Bobby Baker was fundamentally different from that of Senator Williams and Senator Curtis. The senators were two straight arrows in a Senate that was throwing out all the rules to protect individuals. They were no-deals, no-horse-trading, no-negotiated-understandings lone wolves; they weren't going to go along to get along.

On March 8, 1965, Senator Williams gave his opinion about the hearing on the radio program *RPI*:

> Williams started, "I disagree completely with the conclusion of the Committee."
>
> *RPI* responded, "Was it deliberate?"
>
> "Well, they'd have to be deliberate because the Committee had the authority to subpoena the witnesses themselves and call them in.
>
> "They have been more interested in suppressing this and playing it down than they were in developing the facts and there seems to be some fear that it may reflect politically on the administration in power.
>
> "I don't care if it is Republicans or Democrats, and each political party on occasion, I regret to say, have had scoundrels in them. But the administration in power, whether it be Republican or Democrat, when this develops, has a responsibility to the people to expose all of the facts and let them know that whoever is guilty of abusing his public office will be prosecuted and be held accountable. And that has not been done in this case."

Senator John Williams dramatically tossed his "Baker Case" files on the committe table and walked out, charging a whitewash. UPI photo.

Williams remained remarkably bipartisan in his investigative work (most people would say that is lacking on Capitol Hill today ... This country could really use Williams' talents now!). On, April 17, 1965, he spoke to the annual meeting of the American Society of Newspaper Editors. He wanted to continue the investigation to remove any doubt that "someone high in the government" was being protected.

The second Senate report was issued on June 30, 1965. The Committee found McCloskey "candid and convincing" while my uncle's "credibility was totally destroyed" and his testimony "weaved a tortuous path of deception." (My uncle shrugged and said, "They only took a look at what they wanted to.")

The report was riddled with falsehoods: the limits of the Committee were misrepresented, my uncle's testimony was denounced, McCloskey's padding of the performance bond was covered up, and it was untruthfully declared that subpoenas were issued for my uncle in several states.

The Majority had fashioned a story whereby McCloskey and Co. had committed a number of errors, and their agent, Hutchinson, Rivinus & Co., was able to explain away the overcharge. According to the Majority opinion, the overcharge was simply resolved by awarding the $35,000 as general liability insurance to Don Reynolds. My uncle was supposed to turn this payment, minus his commission, over to Rivinus, but the Committee believed that he kept the money for himself. Apparently, Rivinus did get the money; he sent out the bill, as he normally would, to McCloskey, and McCloskey paid it (forgetting they had already paid my uncle).

This comedy of errors apparently legitimized the overcharge. Senator John Cooper from Kentucky wanted to follow up on the discrepancy between my uncle and the Senate Majority. When Senator Cooper asked for documents to substantiate the Majority opinion, Hutchinson, Rivinus & Co. and McCloskey refused to turn over any documents. How's that for corporate accountability?

However, the Minority (three Republican senators) were able to subpoena the coding clerk that received my uncle's invoice. The coding clerk coded the payment to my uncle as 100% performance bond expense for the stadium. If my uncle had indeed been selected to also handle general liability insurance, why was it all coded as performance bond? Maybe it was a mistake, but why did this large overcharge remain without detection by a company auditor for four years? Why did it take a scandal, something from the outside, to make the discovery?

The Minority's report said they couldn't agree with the Committee. In *40 Years Against the Tide*, Senator Curtis wrote, "It is a whitewash, a cover-up, a disgrace to the senators who subscribed to it. It is an endeavor to protect the politically powerful and to make difficult a successful prosecution of Bobby Baker." Curtis also said it well when he said that this Senate report would remain a stain on the country.

Sixty years later, the Senate judgment still stands.

It begs us to ask what we, average citizens elected or appointed to positions of trust, would do in these situations: go against the majority and suffer, or go along to get along? Relationships matter … but the truth does too. Would you vote to protect another senator or the President? What about people you like, people you respect, people you have known all of your life?

In 1965, the Senate turned truth on its head because there was a president involved.

I have come to the conclusion that the jibes and insults reported in the December 1964 edition of *Newsweek* may have been inevitable for a number of reasons. I really don't think there was much room for comity, good will, and understanding; LBJ's tenure and legacy were just too important. The end of the *Newsweek* article summed up the guiding force behind the investigation, "At this point, betting in Washington is about even on whether the full story of the strange case of Bobby Baker and his friends in high places ever will be told."

The truth is a precious commodity, and it is fought over fiercely.

Chapter Ten

The Aftermath

Years ago, a friend told me, "There is our own opinion of ourselves, and also, the opinion of others." For a man like LBJ – a man whom Robert Caro said, "had a bottomless capacity for deceit"; a man whom George Reedy said, "You have to be careful about" ; a man whom RFK said, "was incapable of telling the truth" – to say, "I don't have a thing in the world to hide," sounds more like self-deception than anything else!

Secret recordings don't lie. LBJ was caught on his own tape revealing that he was worried about ending up in jail. The tape of him reacting to the McCloskey hearing in which he states, "Who is going to destroy who?" does not indicate someone who has a clear conscience and peace of mind.

Academics and the U.S. media generally love LBJ. Professor Stanley Kutler from the University of Wisconsin, and Robert Dallek from UCLA (who devoted a mere two paragraphs to the Baker scandal), evidently didn't think the road from Bobby Baker led to LBJ. But it did; it led directly from Bobby Baker to Don Reynolds to LBJ. Robert Caro put it very plainly when he said that the Bobby Baker story became the LBJ story.

If bullets had not reached JFK on the same day that my Uncle Buck had initially testified, all roads would have led to LBJ and resulted in his removal from office, impeachment, and worse.

It's one thing to assert that the President's personality proclivities would lead to unwise decisions for the country. It's quite another to insist there was a planned, devious scheme to subvert constitutional processes. There is consideration of evidence, taken in context and from multiple sources, to suggest that LBJ covered up the investigation, sparked by my uncle, which would have led to the President's resignation, or removal. This is why both Senator Williams and Senator Curtis said there was a strong motivation for a "diabolical scheme" to divert attention from the truth.

Who would win in this battle of the titans: my uncle with Senators Williams and Curtis, or the President with the Senate doing his bidding? History's verdict says that in 1965, LBJ won.

There was only so much Uncle Buck and Senator Williams could do. They had given their all but eventually had to accepted the inevitable. The Senate had assured LBJ's victory in 1964 with their refusal to use Rule19, their refusal to call witnesses, and their belief that my uncle's testimony was "irrelevant." Then, again in 1965, the Senate doubled down with their outrageous report.

***

I often thought about my uncle's courage to confront the President. As a young lad, I had a fascination with the military. I vividly remember watching the old World War II movie *Sink the Bismarck* at the Paramount Theater in Hammond, Indiana. I found it paralleled my uncle's story in an unexpected way.

Bismarck emerged under cloud cover and fog from the Norwegian fjords to engage the British Navy. The British Navy couldn't find her. They tried to guard four exits from the fjords. She was first spotted by air, emerging from the Denmark Strait. Battleships were sent to intercept: HMS *Hood, Prince of Wales,* and other cruisers. Suddenly, a British radio operator at the underground London war room said to the officers assembled, "Signal from *Suffolk*, sir. Have spotted *Hood* and *Prince of Wales,* bearing southeast, distance fifteen miles." A Naval intelligence officer exclaimed, "That mean's they've made it – Good old *Hood*, she'll get them!"

They had cornered the German battleship and the pride of the British Navy would soon end the chase. But instead of capturing the prize, *Hood* was blown up and *Price of Wales* was damaged, fleeing from the battle. It was a bittersweet ending to a military chase that many wished had turned out differently.

All along, our family thought – despite the odds – that the premier investigator and the pride of the Senate, John J. Williams, would chase down and find the truth. He had magnificently done so before. Spurred on from documents and intelligence supplied by my uncle, our family thought Williams would use the information like a torpedo, and the Democratic heavyweight from Texas would be politically "blown up." But just like the officers in the London war room, emotionally entrenched while watching the drama unfold from a distance, our family wished the political chase had turned out differently too.

The battleship *Bismarck* escaped from the Denmark Strait. Sadly, once again with the Senate's imprimatur, Lyndon Baines Johnson also escaped.

During each of those four crises, Uncle Buck came so close to sinking the thirty-sixth President. (There was a good reason that Senator Williams, upon leaving office after four terms in 1978, remarked to his successor, Bill Roth (R, DE), "I had a cabinet full of documents, Bill. We could have taken down the President." And Van Kirk said there was no doubt in his mind that my uncle's documentation would have forced LBJ out of the vice presidency.) My uncle testified against the treacherous Texan at the very moment of his veritable necromanic transformation from persecuted Vice President into the all-powerful President of the United States, and again, he testified on national television in front of the Senate Rules Committee, indirectly implicating Johnson as the sitting President.

It was incredible that at just the right time, someone like Senator John Williams was available to shield my uncle. Even when he got cold feet about testifying, Senator Williams urged him to present himself to the Committee. "I [will] stand by him...." Senator Williams promised, and he did stand by his star witness – not only in the public investigation, but after as well. In the Congressional Record, June 3, 1965, Senator Williams commended not only my uncle, but also my Aunt Jerry and the role she played in this congressional drama.

Williams said:

> I pay my respects not so much to him, although I am glad he testified; I pay my respects to his wife. She is as charming a lady as I have ever met. I have great respect for her. She and Mr. Reynolds were in my office on several occasions. At first, he kept insisting he would not testify and would not produce his records. Finally, his wife was the one who insisted that he had to make a break with the crowd and come clean. She said, "If you do, I will stand back of [behind] you." It was her persuasiveness that induced Mr. Reynolds to talk. I was glad when he turned the records over to us so that we could move ahead, and I am sure he made the right decision.

Then Williams highlighted a problem that plagues us all at one point or another, "When a man has done wrong, he should admit it and clear it up."

In a letter dated June 13, 1965, my Aunt Jerry wrote to Senator Williams' secretary regarding the valiant attempt by the Senator:

> Dear Miss Lenhart,
> Thank you for sending the copies of the Congressional Record. I was very impressed by Senator Williams' remarks and more ap-

preciative than I can tell you for his defense of Don. This has been a battle for the Senator against really overwhelming odds, but I still believe that right will win, rot cannot be covered forever!

Please tell Senator Williams how grateful I am and thank you for your steady friendship.

Best wishes,
Jerry Reynolds

On the program *Opinion in the Capitol*, August 8, 1965, Williams had more praise for my uncle:

> To the extent that I was able to contribute anything toward getting this Baker investigation underway, I owe a lot of that to Mr. Reynolds and his cooperation. I'm not defending Mr. Reynolds. He admitted himself that what he did was wrong, and to use his own language, he told the committee that he acted as a "bagman" – handling some of the political payoffs.
>
> But I was glad that I was able to persuade him not to take the 5th Amendment, but to talk. It is significant that those who are most critical of Mr. Reynolds today, and trying to discredit him, are those who were associating with him in a business way prior to the time that he began to talk. I think the great crime that Mr. Reynolds made in their eyes, is talking.

There were kind words, and great teamwork, but it wasn't enough. The forces of darkness were too great.

In a postmortem of this political battle, Bobby Baker referred to Matt McCloskey and Don Reynolds and said, "I knew what the arrangements (understandings) were." Don Reynolds was indeed the bagman for illegal political payoffs. Baker also said that, "Reynolds told the truth about the DC stadium," the senators "didn't hold [McCloskey's] feet to the fire," and McCloskey never sought to recover the overcharge. *(This last statement was written in Bobby Baker's book.)*

They weren't interested in the truth.

On June 3, 1965, Senator Curtis stated, "The failure of the majority of this committee to diligently pursue this investigation from the very start will stand as a blot on the Senate for all time to come." Senator Williams thought that LBJ was finished, so did my uncle, so did *Life* Magazine assistant editor James Wagenvoord.... "For all time to come" certainly sounds like forever. Today, if you try an electronic search for "LBJ impeachment obstruction of justice," it comes up dry. The Senate judgment has indeed stood for almost sixty years, and the Senate sees no need to correct it. But nothing is truly forever.

Bismarck was eventually disabled by a torpedo, lost its ability to steer, and fell victim to the British fleet. Maybe that Senate judgment will change one day – maybe, as my aunt wrote: the rot will not remain covered forever.

Until his dying day, the President was not bothered again by the outspoken Silver Spring insurance man. LBJ actually emerged from the scandal even stronger than he was before, and he went on the offensive to teach Don Reynolds lessons that would not be forgotten.

Both men responsible for reopening the investigation and finding the truth were about to start new chapters of their lives. John Williams left the Committee room – his services were not needed. The crackerjack investigator had been defeated; he would now view the proceedings from outside the Senate chamber.

In December 1964, Uncle Buck would also view life from an outside perspective. After LBJ won the 1964 election, Uncle Buck was spurred for his fear for his life and departed for Nassau, the capital of the Bahamas where he would live in exile for four years from 1965 to 1969. He wanted to leave the world of Lyndon Johnson and Bobby Baker, and to put his old way of life behind him. Unfortunately, that decision ultimately came with disastrous results.

My Aunt Mary Lou with her brother Don Reynolds in Nassau, circa 1966.

Don Reynolds with prospector Walter Blair, circa 1966.

CHAPTER ELEVEN

THE YEARS OF EXILE AND THE TIMES OF TROUBLE
1964-1968

"Don, we are Masons. I just want to tip you off. Leave the country, leave the States. If you don't, LBJ will have you killed."
–J. Edgar Hoover, head of FBI to Don Reynolds;
as recounted by Don Reynolds to a family friend in 1969

If you talk any more to the attorneys, Williams, or agree to return to the U.S. to testify as a witness, you won't survive."
–Call from Bobby Baker to Don Reynolds in Nassau, February 19, 1966, The John Williams papers, University of Delaware, Newark

"Nassau's gone funky, Nassau's got soul." I listened to those lyrics in my senior year of high school in 1971. Even though it came out two years after my uncle left the Bahamas, I believed it encapsulated a reasonable negotiation for him during four years of exile. He was away from the political heat, he could relax in the sunshine (as he wrote in a postcard to us, "escape the wintry blast"), and do some business. However, his time away turned out to be not so idyllic.

Clark Mollenhoff travelled with Senator Williams to Nassau in September 1965, specifically to talk to my uncle:

Senator Williams stressed that cooperation would make Reynolds look better if an effort was made to prosecute him on tax charges and would avoid the appearance he was running. Reynolds said he was willing, and had been willing, to cooperate but left the States because of continued harassment from the FBI agents, the Rules Committee, and Internal Revenue where the effort seemed to be to get him and let Bobby Baker go his way.

Uncle Buck mentioned to his attorney, James Fitzgerald, he would remain outside the United States until "the present administration and tyranny [was] eliminated." He was prompted to leave because of the farmhouse fire in Oakland, the threatening phone calls he received at his residence on Venetian Road in Silver Spring, and Lyndon Johnson being elected to the presidency. Uncle Buck's business connections were severed. Other friends, and perhaps his own intuition, in consultation with my aunt, convinced him that to some people, his life was not that important. So, he fled, leaving his wife behind in Maryland.

Sardonic questions were asked by more that one person, "Does anybody know what happened to Don Reynolds? Didn't he die in an accident in '64 or '65?"

In the spring of 1967, my family and I had a clandestine visit with Uncle Buck at my Aunt Genevieve's apartment in Washington. We were descending in the elevator to go out to eat when Uncle Buck started talking about security, he ended with: "It costs $347, but it's worth it." At the time, I didn't understand what he was referring to. My mom told me it was a listening device, a bug, that my uncle was considering attaching to his phone in Nassau.

It made sense. For a number of years, my uncle had said publicly to the press that he had received telephone threats. At first, he tried to solve the problem by answering, "Chinese laundry" or, "Grand Central." That wasn't particularly effective, so, Uncle Buck devised his own homemade way to minimize the unwelcomed intrusions. He suggested that we, as family, let the phone ring three or four times, hang up, then call back a couple of minutes later. That way, the odds were, it would be safe for him to pick up.

With his exile, Uncle Buck really thought he had, by location, left a lot of his problems behind. Yet, trouble trailed him mercilessly in full and unrelenting force from' 65 to '69.

Three factors worked against him. My uncle admitted that he was no angel, and neither were his associates. The friends we keep can tell us a lot about ourselves; if we keep company with questionable folk it is very difficult not to adopt some of their practices. We also often take our problems with us and believe that a change of location can erase them. Sometimes that works, but often times, not. And sometimes, those problems take time to develop. In due time, those three conditions would haunt my uncle in Nassau.

Just down the road of life, an official Senate condemnation, as well as marital, business, tax, and legal problems awaited him. And just around the corner in his sunny locale, a special challenge was brewing. Those problems, if they hit concurrently, would have been enough to drive anyone crazy! Uncle Buck could have been likened to Job in the Bible after everything had been taken from him ... or perhaps it was just an example of the inevitable life storms that hit us all. As the Good Book says, "Man is born to trouble as surely as sparks fly upward." –Job5:7

***

In 1965, the New Year started out sunny, but clouds of discouragement were soon hanging low. The lonely years of exile started with an admission: that Uncle Buck had reached his wits' end.

What do you do when you reach the end of your rope? Tie a knot and hang on! Uncle Buck's life-support knot was largely provided by Senator John Williams.

> Emerald Beach Hotel,
> Nassau
> January 4, 1965
>
> Dear Senator Williams,
> Unfortunately, Jerry has not recovered from the long ordeal of harassment and I'm in the process of trying to find a cottage where we can escape the pressure to be applied by the Great Belshazzar [LBJ].
>
> I have never shrunk from the penalty of retribution for any and all transgressions but somehow or other Jerry and I must just survive the tyranny until some semblance of reasonable law and order is followed.
>
> But God forbid that I should offer any help or information to any person where the act of cooperation is considered by the person or body as an excuse to harass, intimidate, and partially destroy the sanity of me or my wife, to continually apply pressure through investigative agencies to undermine my wife, our economic survival, and our very lives.
>
> Senator Williams, the cause to which you have dedicated so much of yourself, your life, and your time is just and right and I hope and trust that God in his infinite wisdom will sustain you and protect you from any harm but the Powers unleashed by the tyrannical acts of King Belshazzar will know no bounds.
>
> I've pretty much reached my wits end Senator Williams, but I do wish you to know that having the privilege of working with and through you and the other two friends we share C & J [Clark Mollenhoff, and Uncle Buck's wife, Jerry] along with H.R.G. [Congressman H.R. Gross from Iowa] has and will remain the most inspiring and satisfying part of my personal endeavor to right the wrongs I know.
>
> Most sincerely,
> Don

My uncle felt the heat of the federal government in its full investigatory power, and his wife's welfare was of great concern to him. Williams offered hope, particularly with the Internal Revenue Service.

> February 23, 1965
>
> Two Internal Revenue agents came in today. The purpose of their meeting was to ask me where they could find Don Reynolds. They said they had been unable to locate him.
>
> I told them I was suspicious – not of them necessarily, but in general – that someone who wanted Mr. Reynolds' testimony out of the way may have interceded or tried to arrange to have Mr. Reynolds disappear; and I asked the question that if he is gone, who would benefit most by his disappearance, and wasn't it possible that someone in a very high position may have engineered his disappearance.
>
> I showed them a copy of the letter where Mr. Reynolds had told the committee of his interest in cooperating – this letter being dated December 1964.

Williams was indeed a lifeline, but my uncle had followed the hearings, and his exasperation mounted.

> 3/8/65
> Dear Senator Williams:
>
> How Almighty God can permit such perversion and deviation of truth as practiced by the Democratic members of the Rules Committee remains a puzzle to me.

As I understand it, he was referring to the second Senate report. The judgment essentially labeled my uncle as a thief, stealing $30,000 (in 1960s dollars), and making up a story that the Senate deemed "unworthy of belief." I can only imagine how depressed it must have made him feel.

In *Reader's Digest*, reporter John Barron recapped the events of the Bobby Baker scandal, "What has happened to the major players in the scandal? Don Reynolds has been ruined. His once profitable insurance business destroyed, he now lives in exile in the Bahamas."[19]

It was true. My uncle had lost his profitable insurance business. The rift was clearly evident from the Equitable Life Assurance Co:

---

[19] "The Case of Bobby Baker and the Courageous Senator," by John Barron, *Reader's Digest* 1966.

October 2, 1964
The Equitable Life Assurance Society of the United States
1285 Avenue of the Americas
New York, New York 10019

Dear Mr. Reynolds:
Please take notice that the Equitable Life Assurance Society of the United States elects to terminate as of seven days from this date, all outstanding Agent's contracts and agreements between yourself and the Society. This action shall not prejudice any continuing rights either party may have thereunder.

Sincerely,
Roy G. Eklund
Senior Agency Vice President

***

In Nassau, my uncle worked with Walter Blair (who discovered yellowcake uranium in Canada). Uncle Buck would often speak glowingly of Walter, saying that he would sleep outdoors in the Canadian cold, and that his adaptability and forthrightness were impressive. Walter Blair's story was told in a *NY Times* article from October 17, 1955 and the book *Sun Dogs and Yellow Cake*. Walt Blair had become fabulously rich and successful.

A few years after the scandal died down, Mollenhoff wanted the rights to his life story:

July 30, 1968
Mr. Walter J. Blair
Hotel Ascot Lavaterstrasse Bahnhoff Enge
Zurich, Switzerland

Dear Walt,
I received your card a few weeks ago, and this week Don has been here briefly for talks with John and me. In addition to our conversations about LBJ and some of the big politics of the moment, we had some further talk about you, your experiences, and the inspiration they might be if put together in a book. In time, I would hope we could get together for some extensive conversations on your life story.

Although our politics are a big upset this year, there is one thing that stands out very clearly: the people are fed up with Lyndon Johnson and his kind of deception and mismanagement of U.S. fiscal affairs and the Vietnam war. It took a long time for them to get wise when all the facts were available, but it does restore my faith in the people of our democracy as far as the long run is concerned. I only hope the damage he inflicted has not been irreparable.

Best to you always,
Cordially,
Clark R. Mollenhoff
940 National Press Building
Washington, DC 20001

Unfortunately, Uncle Buck's working relationship would end sourly with the famous prospector.

***

Senator Williams and Clark Mollenhoff flew to Nassau to update my uncle on developments on the scandal, to assure him that brighter days were ahead, and that Bobby Baker probably would be brought to justice.

Mollenhoff wrote of that trip:

August 4, 1965

Although Don had talked to us periodically over a period of many months, it was obvious that he was pleased to see us. The strain of being an exile was apparent in his comments when we had talked to him on the telephone, and it was obvious that he regarded our visit as more than an opportunity to exchange information about the Bobby Baker investigation and a time for planning the proper moves to make his knowledge available to some honest law enforcement officers. Don regarded the visit as another sign that he was not forgotten and that there were still people who wanted to help him come out of the experience of the Baker investigation with a whole hide.

He carried our bags to the little red Triumph that was parked within a few hundred feet of the air terminal, and even as we walked, he bubbled with enthusiasm over our visit. He wanted us to stay with him at the "Carefree Apartments." Don had his own second floor efficiency apartment, but he had arranged for us to have the use of a four-room apartment owned by an old prospector friend of his, Walt Blair. Blair was out of the city, and Don was eager for us to have the sixth-floor accommodations with the balcony overlooking the beach. We thanked him for his hospitality but told him we wanted to stay at the British Colonial, where we had accommodations reserved. We explained that although we didn't want to say much about our visit with him at this time, we did want to leave a clear record of our visit for his protection and ours.

In the most general terms, we told Don R. that there had been a number of developments in the Bobby Baker case that made us highly optimistic that there would be indictments against Baker and certain that he [Don. R.] would not be indicted. We said we were interested in arranging for him to cooperate with some Justice Department lawyers who we felt were trying to do an aggressive honest job on the Baker case. We said we had been fearful for some time that there would be an effort to make him the goat, and to do little or nothing with Baker. However, we had changed our view in recent weeks and now felt that there were some – and perhaps many who wanted to press forward with the Baker investigation and who felt it would be a bad thing to indict Reynolds, whose cooperation had touched off the first aspects of the whole Baker probe.

We stressed that aside from the Rules Committee Democrats there were few who found the McCloskey version about a $35,000 "goof" to be believable. We stressed that there is considerable independent evidence to show that Baker used others as a conduit in the same way he used Reynolds to obtain cash.

Senator Williams said to my uncle, "Without your help in laying things out, it would have been impossible me to have forced action. Although much of the case went beyond things you told me, we would never have been able to move it without your help."

Despite being buoyed by Williams' and Mollenhoff's visit in August, trouble wasn't far away for my uncle.

Internal Revenue Service District
Director Intelligence Director Intelligence Division
Department of the Treasury

Baltimore, Md
October 8, 1965
Mr. Don B. Reynolds
13122 Venetian Road
Silver Spring, Maryland

Dear Sir:
The current investigation by the Intelligence Division of your income tax liabilities for the years 1960 through 1963 are nearing completion.

Developments of the investigation indicate that a substantial amount of your income is not reflected in your federal income tax returns. Consideration is being given to a possible recommendation that criminal proceedings be instituted against you for attempted evasion of your income taxes, as well as the filing of false and fraudulent income tax returns in behalf of Don Reynolds Associates, Incorporated.

I would presume that my aunt and uncle had not received that letter when she wrote this to me, but the threat of the "T-Men," as she called them, was ever present:

October 10, 1965
Mr. Robert Reynolds Nelson
Munster, Indiana

Hi Darling!
Happy, happy birthday all year long! Don and I have been thinking about you and planning for you this whole month. I went up to Canada to visit with him for a few days before he returned to Nassau. He sends his love to you and your Mom and Dad.

Bobby, we have drawn the money out of the Citizens account in Silver Spring for you. It was made out as a check for Don (as the adult) and I have sent it to him to sign over for you. He will probably send it straight to you from Nassau as soon as he gets it. We wanted it to be added to your account in the bank in your own hometown. Right now, no account of ours is quite safe from the T-Men. Soooo, you'll be getting your birthday present a little bit late this year. OK? Anyway, you know that we have been thinking about you.

I'd love to get a letter from you – and I'll send it right on to Don to read because he is so interested in everything you do.

Give your Mom and Dad a big hug from me. I still feel a little bit out of joint because you were not able to spend some time with me this summer.

Love and kisses,
Aunt Jerry

Every time I read this letter, I marvel at how well my aunt and uncle comported themselves. Perhaps it was because they were my godparents, perhaps it was because they didn't have any children of their own, or maybe it was because my aunt was quite close to my mom. Whatever the reason, they made sure that I didn't feel the effects of the scandal jaws that were threatening to clamp down with finality.

In fact, when we saw Uncle Buck at his Silver Spring house for Thanksgiving in 1965, I remember having a great time. My mom, dad, and I flew TWA out to Friendship Airport in Baltimore, then drove to Silver Spring. I played with Aunt Jerry's and Uncle Buck's two German shepherds outside while the "old folks" talked inside. I don't remember any tension or anything unusual. The big event of that trip for me, according to my mom, was when their dog, Renni, took a bite out of my coat when I was playing in the yard.

Yet, while I had been playing, the owners of the house, with the big yard and the beautiful dogs – my beloved family members – were facing potential prosecution, foreclosure, tax judgments, and physical harm.

Senator Williams had been blocked, and both Walter Jenkins and Matt McCloskey were essentially given free passes. The Senate passed a public judgment, open to any citizen who wanted to read the report, concluding that my uncle had essentially stolen $30,000. It purportedly gave reasons and a logical pathway to why and how he would have done this.

Despite all of that, I had the privilege of feeling secure. My parents provided a loving and protected environment and tried hard to make sure my needs were met. I sensed no danger. In fact, I felt the opposite; to me, life felt stable.

Even though my parents had cultivated a very comfortable bubble for me, my mom knew the dangers that my uncle confronted and fought. She knew it might be time to remind me of some of life's realties. When she saw me making pie-in-the-sky predictions or being lazy, she would remark, "Life isn't always a bowl of cherries, you know."

***

My mom kept a copy of *Despoilers of Democracy* all her life. A letter from Aunt Jerry to the Mollenhoff family showed the closeness of the author and my uncle's cause. I found the letter after my mom had passed away:

> Christmas, 1965
>
> Dear Clark and Mrs. Mollenhoff:
> Don and I want to wish you and your family a joyous Christmas season and of course all the best in the New Year!
> This has been a long year for us, but we have a lot to be thankful for – mainly the steadfast support that you and Senator Williams have given us both. We are both so grateful to you for your interest and friendship.
> As part of my Christmas greeting to our friends, I am encour-

aging them to get your book, *Despoilers of Democracy*. Don's three sisters are also spreading it around in Georgia, Chicago, and Washington. If it doesn't sell a million copies, it won't be because we haven't tried.

While Aunt Jerry kept connections healthy on the home front, Uncle Buck found his situation in exile deteriorating despite his efforts to escape his troubles.

This never-before-published letter from my uncle to Senator Williams shocked me; it detailed a threat from Bobby Baker.

March 6, 1966

On February 19, 1966, at some time between 1:30-2:00 AM, I was awakened by the telephone ringing in my apartment in Nassau.

The operator connected me with a person who said, "This is Bobby Baker and I am making one more effort to protect myself from further difficulties brought about by you talking to John Williams and the two attorneys appointed by the Justice Department for the prosecution of my case."

Bobby said, "You'd better believe me – if you do not take heed, just remember, you hope to return to the U.S. someday and that he, Black, Webb, and Don Murchison have friends who would have me physically taken care of." Bobby said, "Don, you have caused problems for some big men. What is done is done and they have survived without too many problems. They are willing to forget the whole mess, but this is my final warning to you, from myself and from them: if you talk any more with the attorneys, Williams, or agree to return to the U.S. to testify as a state witness – you won't survive."

If I tried to double-cross him by informing anyone of his offer to help, he would know about it. That Cohen had informed him, through friends, that FBI and Justice had coordinated on me and that I'll probably get 49 years in prison for fraud-perjury and other charges. Bobby has made other wild claims in the past, so I wasn't too worried but now I am.

I had very little chance to comment as I was caught so unaware, but I inferred that he did not frighten me (even though he did).

Senator, I left Nassau in such a manner that I was not sure I would return, and at the moment, I am suspended in midair in Canada. Truthfully, I guess that I am a bit frightened, not only of LBJ's power, but also the threat of physical violence to me… I feel terribly afraid and alone; even though I'm sure of you, Clark, and Jerry, it may be beyond your powers to help.

Thanks so much for your sincerity, and your long hard hours of work to help uncover this horrible mess and to expose it. If I don't survive, please understand that I know you did everything you could, and for that, I am deeply indebted to you – the same as all decent Americans are debtors to you...

I plan to be here another 10 days unless I get some indication that I need not fear Bobby's threats, but if I don't get some reassurance, I'll have to travel on.

Sincerely,
Don

This was coming from a man who *never* admitted weakness. With Baker's unexpected phone call and a continual stream of threats, Nassau didn't feel like a big enough town to hide in, or far away enough to be safe. Uncle Buck had tried to escape the physical and emotional heat, but he had been unsuccessful.

Two months earlier, Baker had been indicted by a grand jury and his options were drying up. (He never wrote about the indictment in his memoirs). I believe his threats were merely an attempt to intimidate – to restrict the range of verbal and written ability of my uncle to inflict further serious damage to Baker, who was about to be judged and sentenced. My uncle, the man whom Baker had helped get rich, had turned him in. In Baker's view, it was a clear case of biting the hand that feeds you.

***

In the summer of 1966, all of our family (my mother, father, aunts, and uncles) took a trip to Canada. We met Uncle Buck in Windsor, the Canadian city across from Detroit. I'll never forget the good times we had there together as a family, but more poignantly, I remember standing on the second floor balcony of a motel with a solemn Uncle Buck. We stood together and stared out across the Detroit River. In a pensive moment, his gaze narrowed on the skyscrapers in the downtown area of the American city. He paused longingly as he thought about his exile. He looked at me and said, "No, no. I can't go back."

Then, after that special family rendezvous, marital trouble attacked what little stability Uncle Buck had left in his life.

From Senator Williams' personal records:

September 14, 1966

I received a telephone call from Don Reynolds last night shortly after 11 PM.

He has been in California and had spent several days trying to find Jerry to try effecting a reconciliation. He learned through a lawyer that represents her that she and her mother have gone to Nevada, apparently for the purpose of establishing residence prior to a divorce.

Reynolds said that the lawyer informed him that Jerry had been approached by a number of federal agents in recent weeks and they had indicated to her that they still intended to prosecute Reynolds and that the only way she could avoid prosecution would be to separate from him.

Reynolds was considerably distraught about not being able to find Jerry but decided there was probably nothing he could do about it now and plans to return to Canada where he will get back to work and try to forget about it until such time as other things have settled down. He seemed considerably depressed over the fact that he had been unable to talk to Jerry to even try to effect a reconciliation. He was also concerned over the indications that the Justice Department or the Internal Revenue was still trying to prosecute the case despite the fact that prosecution was not recommended at a lower level.

But this was not the end; the storms just seemed to be getting stronger.

The Senate had not cleared my uncle, but Senator Williams and Clark Mollenhoff had teamed up in an effort to convict Baker. (They thought of themselves as the real-life equivalent of Perry Mason and the investigator, Paul Drake, on *Perry Mason*.) Baker had seen it coming when he said, "John Williams is] going to get us all in jail." But he had only been half right. Baker was the sacrifice so that LBJ would not be touched.

In January of 1967, Bobby Baker was charged, tried, and finally convicted of a number of crimes, principally stealing money from his friend, Senator Robert Kerr – money that was supposed to go for lobbying efforts for the savings and loan industry. So, in the end, Williams and Mollenhoff had not been totally defeated, but because of a number of appeals, Baker would not go to jail until 1971.

Bill Bittman was the lead attorney in the government's case against Baker. In a revealing archive from Senator Williams' collection, Bittman talked about my uncle and the trial. He was highly appreciative of Don Reynolds, but gave thumbs down to the FBI and the DOJ.

> In commenting on Reynolds, Bittman said that as a former government official, he was ashamed of the deliberate attempt which the FBI, under the instructions of the Department of Justice, went out

of it way to smear and discredit Reynolds as a prospective witness against Baker. The manner in which the questions by the FBI were asked of the various people interrogated could produce nothing but charges of Reynolds being a liar, etc. For example, in Reynolds' testimony about the wild parties which certain individuals attended, the FBI's investigation did not conclude if such a party was held or if the mentioned people attended, but rather, Reynolds was asked, if on a certain night, certain individuals had an illicit affair with some woman. Automatically, his answers were, 'No.' Therefore, the assumption was drawn that Reynolds was a liar. In Mr. Reynolds' statement, he had not charged that these men had slept with the women, but merely that it was a wild party attended by so and so.

How can we have confidence in our government, confidence in the idea of self-government, with judgments like this?

***

In April of 1967, we took a trip to Washington, DC to visit my Aunt Genevieve and Uncle Ross. Although Uncle Buck was still living in exile in the Bahamas at the time, he was in attendance too. I had a habit of taking my tape recorder everywhere with me, and I remember interviewing my uncle. "The day is April 20, 1967 and my Uncle Buck is here. What do you have to say?"

Uncle Buck responded, "Well, I'm particularly pleased today since you folks are here. But I'm surprised it's the 20th. I'm supposed to be somebody else today, some other place." (This was his indirect way of saying that, at a minimum, he was supposed to be in the Bahamas, not Washington, D.C.)

There was a comic moment of relief as he changed the subject, "[Bobby], I hear you have some new ideas on becoming a father ..." He proceeded to recount an anecdote from my youth. According to Uncle Buck, (although I really don't remember saying this), when I was younger, I had believed I would achieve fatherhood while my future wife was asleep. My uncle, emphasizing he knew the truth, chimed, "I know the real horse."

I indignantly responded, "I didn't say that; I can assure you."

To which Uncle Buck replied, "I don't know about that, I think the horse is going to come up and tell us." This was the cryptic, roundabout way of getting a point across that my uncle was often fond of using.

The family fun ended and we went back to Indiana, but unbeknownst to me, the T-Men were knocking at Uncle Buck's home in Silver Spring. Judging from the records from the Treasury Department, it might have been better had he not opened the door. Perhaps it shouldn't have been a surprise. (LBJ was heard on the secret presidential tapes advising Sheldon Cohen, IRS Commissioner, to "get tough with Reynolds." And Sheldon Cohen did exactly that.)

On April 12, 1967, two letters were set by Cohen to Mr. Don B. Reynolds and Mrs. Geraldine M. Reynolds, Silver Spring, Maryland and Mr. and Mrs. Reynolds, Nassau, Bahamas. The two letters indicated unpaid tax and penalties for the years of 1960 and 1963.

The Minneapolis Star Tribune told the story in 1967:

> The Internal Revenue Service has levied a claim for $174,000 against Don B. Reynolds, the Maryland insurance man who was a key figure in exposing the activities of Robert G. (Bobby) Baker.
>
> Reynolds, formerly a business associate of Baker, said Saturday that "the Johnson Administration has been hounding me and my wife for more than three years, and now they are going to try to break me."
>
> The former insurance man said that Internal Revenue Commissioner Sheldon S. Cohen's Department is "trying to credit me with more than $100,000 income, when the money was actually collected for Bobby Baker's use through overpayments of insurance premiums by the Carpenter's Union."
>
> Reynolds said that although he received the money, it was not for his personal use. "I received my normal insurance commissions, and I reported them as income. I took the overpayments and put them in my 'hanky-panky' bank account that I used in dealing with Baker. It was there to be used for his benefit and under his direction, and when I bought stock in my name it was on behalf of Baker and other political people… I was just working as Baker's pay-off man.

For every action, there is a reaction. This prosecution by the IRS probably precipitated the following letter to Clark Mollenhoff, indicating a double-cross. It was not from my uncle, but rather Walt Blair, the famous prospector with whom my uncle had worked.

> Hotel Zurich
>
> Dear Clark Mollenhoff:
> In reference to Don Reynolds, I have done the guy only good but in turn he double-crossed me by stealing my cheques and forging my signature and cashing them. He cashed two cheques in Toronto, the third one they turned him down, and one cheque in Swiss Credit Bank, Switzerland for sf109,000 and I don't exactly know

what he took out of my account in Toronto when I had some $30,000 there.

I am going to bring the same Don Reynolds to justice if it is the last thing I do. He is a CON man and a real thief. I think you should revise your book on what Don Reynolds said and write a new book exposing your error and Don Reynolds. I am sorry I have to do this, but I am going to save others and expose that bastard.

I am on my way back to the Bahamas to pick up the cheque that he forged my account with.

Sincerely,
Walter Blair

Uncle Buck had committed his second felony. I imagine the tax pressure was too great for him to bear.

Then, Aunt Jerry's resigned resolve to leave Uncle Buck was made clear in her letter to my Aunt Mary Lou in Georgia:

June 4, 1967

My dear Mary Lou,
Nearly a year has gone by since I came home, and I cannot believe it! The changes, of course, have been dramatic, but at this perspective and point in time, I believe I can see more clearly – certainly less emotionally than at any time in the past year. I have missed being able to talk to you – to tell you about what is happening and how I feel, as we did weekly, the year and a half I was alone. I often think about Don – wondering where he is – how he is – what he is doing, and I pray that things are beginning to take shape for him again, as they have for me. Although I have had moments of panic when I wished I could undo all that has been done, I am more certain than ever now that our separation was inevitable because Don needs his freedom.

Whatever the case, Mary Lou, now that the year is behind us, I'd love to correspond occasionally – to hear about you and Dot and the cats – and all the rest of the family, too – including Don. I can now receive mail at General Delivery, Los Osos, California.

Love,
Jerry

My father and I were working outside on our lawn in Munster in the summer of 1967. My mom came out of the house and said, "Buck and Jerry are getting a divorce." My dad turned his head in disgust and said,

"It doesn't surprise me." There was a great deal of antipathy between him and my uncle. Even if Don Reynolds was the "Star Witness," he certainly wasn't a star as far as my dad was concerned.

On November 9, the IRS and Sheldon Cohen upped the ante with my aunt, sending out bills to her in Silver Spring. They stipulated that the amounts owed were $146,201.71 for 1960 and $56,930.41 for 1963.

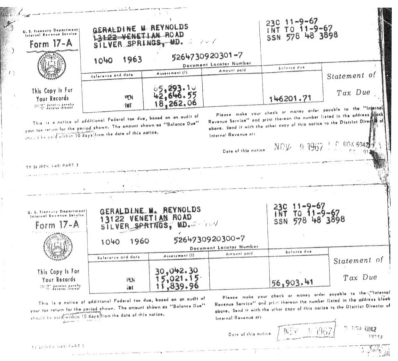

The 1960 and 1963 IRS tax judgments sent to my uncle's 2nd wife.

1968 should have started as A Happy New Year, but it was not so happy for Walt Blair; Uncle Buck had been stealing money from his former friend's bank account again.

> January 3, 1968
> Park View Hotel
> Durban, South Africa
>
> Dear Mr. Mollenhoff:
> I presume you heard of the letter I wrote to Senator Williams re: Don Reynolds.
> I think this man Reynolds should see a psychiatrist – he is going mental.

He is a real con man; he doesn't think twice about signing my name to cheques he stole out of my bank books.

The National Bank of Florida turned down a cheque for $2,750.00 he signed my name to.

Don is a dangerous man – he can't go straight, and the end results will be the same as the rest of things.

I just want to tip you off.

Yours truly,

This was my uncle's third felony. Uncle Buck did not share his internal and emotional life, and my aunt never shared any of this side of the story with me either. I assume it is true. I don't know whether my uncle ever paid Walter Blair back, but I like to think that he did. I still can't help but wonder, *was my uncle a con artist? Who was the real Don B. Reynolds?* When I visited Oakland in 2020, his neighbor, Dan Beckman, called him a "shyster." So, perhaps the better question is, who was the better shyster: Don Reynolds or LBJ?

On November 4, 1968, it finally felt like everything was going to change for the better. I remember walking home from cross country practice, then getting a call from Uncle Buck: Richard Nixon had defeated Hubert Humphrey. We cheered with the change in administration. There was a sense of relief in his voice; the long ordeal, the lonely years of exile were over. His long nightmare was at an end … or was it?

May 1, 1969
Mr. Walter Blair
Nassau, The Bahamas

Dear Mr. Blair:
The things you have written about the activities of Don Reynolds have caused the deepest sorrow. Initially I had hoped that was some mistake or misunderstanding of Don's actions, for I have wanted to believe that he had reformed since first telling Senator John Williams about his dealings with Bobby Baker and others. We knew and understood something about his past but hoped there had been a genuine reformation.

 Senator Williams and I have talked about the contents of your letters, and the Senator is as disappointed as I am over the distressing story you relate. There is no justification for anyone doing the things you say he has done with your accounts. This is particularly true when it represents a misuse of the funds of someone who has been as good a friend as you have tried to be.

The pressures of his tax problems as well as the harassment by the Johnson Administration have been factors in his action, I am sure. However, he is an adult, should know better, and will have to take the consequences of his actions.

Neither Senator Williams nor I would want you to do anything other than pursue honest prosecution of your rights. We regret it has turned out this way, for we have wanted to believe the best about him.

Fortunately, the prosecution of Bobby Baker was unrelated to any testimony or evidence from Don, so that conviction will rise or fall on its own independent merits. The story that Senator Williams told was heavily corroborated on most major points, and I have always been careful in weighing what Don has told me because of the problem of credibility that arose out of his earlier operations with Bobby Baker. Thanks for the information even though it has been a shock to learn of your experience.

Sincerely yours,
Clark Mollenhoff

Mollenhoff did confirm that, as far as he was concerned, my uncle's testimony was valid. But, every so often, as soon as you think you understand another person, a shocking truth can upend everything. Can we accept the same with LBJ – there was a dark side to him that the American populace never fully understood?

Our notion of self-government is based on virtues – that the truth will be told. Without truth, integrity erodes. We become divided, suspicious, thinking the worst of any situation and our fellow man. (I can't help but see striking parallels to today.)

There was no denying the two Senate judgments and the haunting four year record. The Senate condemnation was permanently etched, he had received threats of violence, and even more importantly, a powerful president had vowed revenge against him. Uncle Buck's wife was gone, his house went to foreclosure, he had no children, his business was liquidated, he had a huge tax bill, and prosecution was looming.

In the end, Don Reynolds was unable to break free; he unjustly remained a prisoner of his own tortured political past. He passed away in August of 1993. However, his last twenty-five years shed some light on his actions and the inevitable surprising judgments that history would bring to not only him, but to Bobby Baker, the U.S. Senate, and LBJ.

CHAPTER TWELVE

25 YEARS OF FAMILY SECRETS
1968-1993

It was 1972, and the crucial day had arrived. As a favor, Mike Buckley (who lived on my dorm floor), promised to record and relay everybody's numbers for the draft. I had gotten back from class, and the moment of truth for nineteen-year-olds had arrived. I was understandably nervous.

"Let's see, Nelson, Nelson…"

The seconds seemed like minutes. "*Mike!* What is it?"

"Well, Bob, you'd better sit down." I did not like that answer.

In honest disbelief, I yelled, "*Mike!*"

"342, Nels, 342." Buckley, who had a reputation as a practical joker, had had his few seconds of fun at my expense.

I had briefly thought I would be receiving an all-expense paid trip from the government to a rice paddy in the People's Republic of Vietnam, courtesy of none other than LBJ.

At that same time, Bobby Baker was receiving his all-expense paid, sixteen-month trip to Lewisburg, Pennsylvania Federal Prison. Baker was paying for his crimes. There were events in newspapers, and longer articles in magazines, but at that time, my vision was narrower; I was just intent on my studies and not having to carry a gun.

My own tunnel vision, and the reticence of my family to talk about the scandal, made the two and a half decades before Uncle Buck's death a puzzling, enigmatic, and surreal time. Family gatherings, photos, and conversations all seemed to indicate that if there was a past scandal, it was all over and done with.

The closing of the Gold Window, Whip Inflation Now (the government's program offering anti-inflationary initiatives), the Vietnam War, Nixon's entrée to China, Watergate, Iran-Contra, détente, and the fall of the Berlin Wall all happened during this quarter century, from 1968-1993. While those events were making deep impressions on the average citizen, I believed, and our family hoped, that the Baker scandal would quietly get swept into the dustbin of history. Where my family wanted to remain mum about the whole scandal, Bobby Baker would eventually decide to tell his story.

***

In 1973, during summer vacation between my sophomore and junior year, my mom had excitedly announced, "Aunt Jerry's going to have a baby with her new husband!" At age 48, she naturally birthed her daughter, Mindy. The same year that my aunt was giving birth to life, the Grim Reaper took out the most pivotal player in the Bobby Baker scandal: Lyndon Baines Johnson.

***

In 1974, my uncle got married for the third time to a woman named Ingrid Luttert. I remember the phone conversation when he announced the big news. He said the lady he was marrying wasn't a model, she was "zurückgehalten" (meaning "reserved" or "quiet" in German) a verb meaning "to hold back," but that he truly felt close to her. At the time, I had no idea of Aunt Ingrid's connection to the Baker scandal – she had actually taken the stand in the Senate hearings on the Baker scandal in December 1964!

Aunt Ingrid was born in northern Germany in a town called Bielefeld. My uncle had met her parents as a counselor officer while in Berlin, so he briefly knew her as a child. In the 1960s, while he was working in the Defense Department, she worked in Germany's Defense Ministry as a secretary for Helmut Schmidt, the leader of West Germany. Later, she went to the UK to study English.

Aunt Ingrid met Ellen Romestch, a German model, on the boat coming over to the States in 1960. Once in the U.S., they roomed together. Romestch had relationships with high-powered people in Washington. According to Bobby Baker, the Elizabeth Taylor-look-a-like had relationships with Gerald Ford, and of all people, JFK. (During the Profumo scandal in the UK, Attorney General Bobby Kennedy whisked Rometsch out of the U.S. because the national security implications were running high.)

Senator Williams later went to Aunt Ingrid's apartment for an interview on the Baker scandal. She had moved out of the house where she and Rometsch were staying, saying, "Elly's doing this for money, and I just can't stand it." She also told Senator Williams, "I know things I don't want to know."

All of these developments probably endeared Ingrid to my uncle. They had shared numerous political hills, valleys, and winding roads during the scandals. Life experiences matter, and they had both been through a lot. Uncle Buck and Aunt Ingrid both knew where the bodies were buried. It seemed that a deep understanding was established between them based on their common experiences and worldview.

(I was vacationing at my Aunt Mary Lou's home in Augusta, Georgia when I happened to come upon *The Bobby Baker Affair: How to Make Millions in Washington* by G.R. Schreiber. The author mentioned a woman named Irene Luttert, who worked for the World Bank, just like Aunt Ingrid. Although the names didn't match, I casually asked my Aunt Mary Lou, "What was Ingrid's maiden name?" I'll never forget where I was in the house and the sound of her voice when she answered "Luttert." The name seemed to float across the kitchen. It was a moment that I would always remember – the moment I discovered a hidden truth. To me, it was a subtle, unspoken confirmation of the code my family had been living by: *I hope you won't ask, because I really don't want to tell.*)

We had good times with Uncle Buck and Aunt Ingrid, particularly at the beach at Hilton Head Island. My uncle remained married to her until his death in 1993. My mom once said, "It did work. The only thing that irritated Buck was when they would go out to a restaurant, and Ingrid would be mistaken for his daughter."

My mom and Aunt Ingrid stayed close, even after Uncle Buck had passed. They both visited my home in DeForest, Wisconsin in 2017. Though I was considering writing this book at that time, I just couldn't bring myself to ask about her role in the scandal; the family code had been deeply ingrained in me.

***

Bobby Baker's book *Wheeling and Dealing* came out in 1978. I don't remember our family discussing it (or any other publications from 1968-1993 for that matter). Everything went below the waves ... but secrets don't usually stay sunk forever.

In the early 1980s, I was working on the West Coast in Portland, Oregon. One day, I decided to reward myself by visiting a Portland institution: Powell's Bookstore. I was meandering through the stacks of treasures when all of a sudden, the past caught up to the present. I saw *Wheeling and Dealing*. It was like forbidden fruit. I almost felt like a teenager finding a father's hidden *Playboy* magazine. No one had told me that Bobby Baker, the man in the spotlight, had written a book.

On the back cover, the famed political columnist Jack Anderson, wrote, "May well be the political publishing event of 1978." I scanned down the index, looking for "R" ... There it was, "Reynolds, Don."

I applied in 1983 to the CIA as an imagery analyst at the National Photographic Interpretation Center in Washington. I took the test, wrote an essay, and then went for an interview at the Washington Navy Yard. The job didn't pan out in the end, but a friend gave me some words of explanation, "Once they found out your middle name was Reynolds, and you told them you were reading *Wheeling and Dealing*, they could pretty well fill in the picture."

Frankly, I enjoyed the book, and I recommend it. It was bereft of documentation, but Baker's relationship to LBJ had some amusing moments. Commenting on an ambassador Chester Bowles, LBJ said, "He's losing us friends all over the world with his goddamned halitosis. I got a whiff of it the other day and if it had been Khrushchev instead of me, there'd likely be a war on now."

LBJ also remarked about John Connally leaving the Democratic Party, "It's embarrassing to me. Now, hell, John could sneak around and vote Republican, but he didn't need to beat his breast and yodel like Tarzan."

Baker's retelling of his 16 month stretch in prison was revealing, if only to expose his attitude toward my uncle and Senator Williams. After all, it was my uncle that set the ball rolling on the whole Baker affair, which ultimately landed Baker behind bars.

One name stands out in Baker's account of his time in Lewisburg Prison. It was the name of a man with whom my uncle had actually done business with, but whom Baker had only met while at Lewisburg: Jimmy Hoffa, the famed union boss.

Baker relied on Hoffa's protection to survive, whereas my uncle knew him from a failed development (using Teamster's pension funds) in Jacksonville, Florida called WERTCO.

Upon Baker's arrival to prison, Hoffa said, "You ain't anybody in here, Bobby. Your ass belongs to the gypsies. Uncle Sam couldn't care less what happened to it."

"Why?" asked Baker.

"You represent the Establishment to these guys. You represent authority to them. You represent the enemy."

In Baker's book, the chapter called "Surviving in the Slammer" retells a story about "Big Al," and Hoffa's role in preserving Baker's life.

Big Al, a magnificent physical specimen (as Baker described him) and a cold-blooded murderer, had been released from Leavenworth Prison to see if he would be eligible for parole. He was transferred to Lewisburg, and assigned to Baker's kitchen detail.

Problems arose quickly; Big Al was not performing his duties properly. Baker went back to his barracks, and Big Al followed him. "You motherfuck. Me gonna kill you," said Al. After that, a temporary, uneasy peace was established; however, according to Baker:

> Big Al got on my case again. He muttered threats through the noon work shift, gave me the hard eye, and finally a throat-cutting gesture. I'd had enough, so I called him a Spanish word I loosely understood to mean cocksucker. Apparently, that's exactly what it meant. Big Al went up in flames. It took a half-dozen inmates to restrain him. I armed myself with a stack of heavy metal trays until he'd been calmed and led away.
>
> – Bobby Baker in Lewisburg Prison; from his book *Wheeling and Dealing*, 1978

Hoffa's confidant, Jake Ursini, said to Baker, "Big Al's gone apeshit. I've managed to keep you alive because I keep telling him that you're tight with Hoffa, but even that won't work if you keep on insulting him."

Baker said, "Look, I'm afraid of that big bastard. I know he's a killer. Hell, he's proven it! But I can't let him abuse me and kick me around like a dog."

The end of the story resulted in Ursini confiscating "a wickedly long knife with a curved point," while Big Al was hiding in the grass waiting for Baker.

I can hardly imagine what it must have been like for Baker, living through these experiences as he got into his golden years.

Renowned historian, Arthur Schlesinger, reviewed Baker's book; "Bobby Baker's Senate is composed of crooks, drunks, and lechers, marching from bar to boudoir to bank, concerned mainly with lining their pockets and satisfying their appetites."

Perhaps, just as significant for our family, Schlesinger then noted the Baker-Reynolds-LBJ-Watergate connection: "Mr. Baker does insist, however, that had he told the whole truth about the kickback Mr. Johnson received from Don Reynolds in return for a life insurance policy, the result would have been to 'torpedo the Vice President. These revelations...

could have denied him the Presidency, or driven him from office like Richard M. Nixon'"

– Historian Arthur Schlesinger, *New York Times,* May 28, 1978.

This confirmed the contention that the Baker scandal was LBJ's scandal. *My uncle made that possible!*

CHAPTER THIRTEEN

DON REYNOLDS – CRUDE OR COMPASSIONATE?

Who was Don Buck Reynolds? I hate to say it, but the words "crude, rude, and lewd" could be used to describe aspects of my uncle's personality.

The Pentagon report said that Reynolds was quick to turn on people who he said had double-crossed him, and that he had not gotten the trust of his State Department staff. There was also some comment that Reynolds liked to exaggerate and embellish certain stories.

I searched my memories to discover if these statements were true within his familial interactions.

On August 15, 1971, the U.S. was taken off the gold standard – severing the dollars convertibility to gold at $35/ounce. On that same day, I was staying with my Aunt Mary Lou. I called Uncle Buck on the phone, and asked what was going on. He said, "All hell has broken loose!" (My aunt said Uncle Buck always loved to try to shock me.) I mentioned what my dad had thought about gold and its volatility, to which he replied, "Your dad is the average American businessman who knows absolutely nothing about international affairs and economics." After I shared his opinion with my mom, she said, "Oh, please, don't tell your father!"

Uncle Buck would often say, "The dollar is finished." That didn't appear to come to fruition, but my Aunt Mary Lou bought some gold on his recommendation and profited handsomely. She would later say, "You know, he was right about certain things," referring to gold's meteoric rise after 1971.

Uncle Buck and his sister, Mary Lou, had a special bond, yet Buck would occasionally make disparaging comments about his brother, Reginald. Sometimes, I couldn't tell if it was a joke or a blatant dig, but one obvious jibe took place at my Uncle Reginald's house in Lamar. The conversation got very heated between the two men, at which point, my Aunt Ingrid quietly remarked, "Well, it's time for us to go now…"

Again, Reginald was the target at our Hilton Head beach gathering. We had a party of eight people, and one check. A discussion occurred about how the bill should be split. Somehow, we couldn't solve the dilemma. Then, in a decisive tone of voice, Uncle Buck came to the rescue. With a muted laugh directed to me, he said, "Sign it all to Reginald's name. That ought to kill him."

Uncle Buck and his family seemed to live in different worlds. Indeed that divergence in worldview was apparent when Uncle Buck walked into Uncle Reginald's small-town shoe store in Darlington, South Carolina, with a copy of *Euromoney* in his hand. The scene was completely incongruous.

***

In the summer of 1978, I visited Uncle Buck at his Washington apartment on Van Ness Street. He showed me a copy of the *Washington Post* front-page story about Peter Bourne, President Carter's health czar, and the drug treatment scandal. What ensued was Uncle Buck's summary of the world's problems and Watergate. "I don't trust the Germans, Bob. That's the problem this government has had. Too many Germans! Haldeman, Ehrlichman…"

Then, with a sideways glance he said, "Bob, would you like to meet John Dean?"

I froze. I could only imagine what kind of conversation I might have with the attorney responsible for covering up Watergate, who later shared his testimony to bring down Nixon.

My uncle earnestly persisted, "Would you like to meet him?"

"Well, yeah," I said, "What's he doing now?"

"Stockbroker."

A ten-minute phone conversation ensued between Uncle Buck and John. Uncle Buck hung up the phone and said, "Good. You'll get to meet him."

The next day, through summer heat, humidity, and low visibility, in one of Washington's many traffic circles, I saw a bespectacled man walk toward my uncle's Mercedes. I didn't recognize him. The man got in the car and we made our introductions. After five minutes of conversation, my uncle remarked, "John, Bob thought you were *the* John Dean!" He slapped his knee as he laughed.

I don't deny a certain amount of naïveté on that one, but looking back, I should have guessed. Uncle Buck was a man who really wanted to forget the past. He never once mentioned the book, *Wheeling and Dealing*, or its author – the man with whom he worked for so many years who lived on his same avenue in Washington, DC.

Uncle Buck saw me off at Washington National with a simple political farewell, "Say hello to Mayor Daley for me."

***

As any individual, he had his faults as well as his strengths. As he worked in insurance, Uncle Buck demonstrated a habit of saving documents. As such, he had a lesson for me when I met him and his wife, Ingrid, at Hilton Head after I returned to the States from my 1983 trip to Israel and Egypt. My Aunt Mary Lou had saved my mail while I was on the trip. When I opened up my credit card statement at the beach hotel where we were staying, I was shocked. Uncle Buck asked what the matter was. I said, "Well, this can't be right … a dinner in Alexandria cost me $606.00!" He asked, "Did you save the receipt?" (The dinner was actually $6.06. It was a simple matter of zeros that was resolved in due time.) Since then, I have always been careful to keep my receipts! To me, his habit confirmed his claims about the Bobby Baker affair.

It held him in good stead on the History Channel too. As Burkett Van Kirk, Republican Minority lead counsel said on the documentary *Kennedy vs. Johnson Chasing Demons*, "Everything [Don] said, he had a receipt for. It's hard to argue with a receipt, or an invoice, or a cancelled check. It's hard to argue with documentation."

Was Uncle Buck hard on people? He could be. At that same beach vacation, I can remember him watching President Reagan talking about an issue on TV. Uncle Buck remarked, "Look at him. Stupid!"

***

The report from the columnist, Jack Anderson, also mentioned that Don Reynolds had made antisemitic remarks as a consular officer in Berlin.

I still remember a joke that Uncle Buck felt was appropriate to share with me. "Bob, what was the fastest things on wheels in the 1930s?"

"Uh, a Porsche?" I responded warily.

"A Jew on a bicycle trying to get out of Germany."

Another time, I had mentioned that Pierre Salinger (Johnson's press secretary after Bill Moyers) had come to the university as a guest speaker.

My uncle remarked, "That kyke from California! Got into some phony land deals out there."

***

He also loved to take physical risks, or more simply, to show off. One time, he was driving my mom and dad through southern Germany, zipping around hairpin curves through the mountains. He was driving at least fast enough to scare the wits out of my dad. To my uncle, it was familiar territory, and besides, he was driving a Mercedes, but to my dad, it might as well have been the updated version of Jan and Dean's "Dead Man's Curve."

Suddenly, there was a loud sound from the back seat. My dad, in frustration, had thrown his camera on the floor of the car. He had really had it.

That incident was remembered and retold for a long time. There was no small degree of animosity between my dad and my uncle.

As a family, we prayed for peace, limited interactions, and hoped for the best.

***

Uncle Buck made controversial statements about sex.

In 1967, he came to Augusta, Georgia, where my Aunt Mary Lou lived, and announced to the family that sex was a priority item because we are "born in sex." His comments about sex and religion brought his sister to her limit. She lashed out in frustration, "Buck, you're an old man!"

"No, I'm not, Mary Lou."

Pointing towards me, she said, "Look, he's a young man. You're an old man!"

He later tried to get a transatlantic romance going between a German girl, Elvira, and me. She was the daughter of the woman he was dating at the time. The girl's picture was prominently displayed on my desk at home, and we exchanged letters in German. Then, suddenly the letters stopped. My uncle explained matter-of-factly that the attractive fräulein had caught the attention of a Luftwaffe officer.

***

My uncle had a huge tax bill. A friend of the family remembers seeing what he believed to be a copy of a tax lien document in my uncle's hand. As far as he knew, my uncle did not have the resources to pay off the lien. If the saying, "Nothing can be said to be certain, except death and taxes" is true, then the only way to solve the problem was to have the former occur to extinguish the later. This is what happened in the case of IRS vs. Don B. Reynolds.

***

There was more than one facet to Don Reynolds; there was no doubt that he also felt relaxed around family. He could be sure that he would not be taken advantage of; there were no blind corners that he had to be wary of. One time, while in my Aunt Mary Lou's home, he noticed one of her two cats reclining on a pillow on a couch, paws outstretched. He turned to me and said, "You know, I wish I could relax like that."

He once mentioned that he wanted to tell me more about his views on life, and perhaps to hear mine in return, but he "didn't want to say anything to create a problem." He was probably indirectly referencing my mom, and even more so, my dad.

Aunt Mary Lou mentioned that Uncle Buck had a chance encounter at a Washington department store with Baker, but that was it. There would be no more news articles, interviews, or TV appearances for the Star Witness of the Baker scandal. There would also be no documents, or any personal effects from my uncle or the scandal, that survived the test of time. After all he had been through, I guess he just wanted things to remain unimportant.

I believe there were a number of reasons that culminated in his eventual silence regarding the scandal: The death threats and menacing phone calls that continued into the '70s and '80s, Baker and Uncle Buck living on the same street in Washington, Uncle Buck's third wife working for the World Bank, he didn't want to involve his larger family in the aftermath of the scandal, the guilt and shame over his past actions, the Senate condemnation and all the problems that came with fighting that, and his desire to just enjoy his retirement – continuing to be in the public eye wasn't worth it.

Uncle Buck had been made the scapegoat, the one who took the blame for everything that went wrong with the scandal. Just as he feared: after all was said and done, he remained on the outside as the pariah, the odd man out, the patsy for everything.

I think he ultimately just gave up. "I'm too old to get involved with this," was his attitude near the end, "I've fought the good fight, done more than was expected … I'm not physically harmed. It's time to move on."

The last time I talked with him was in December of 1992 when my wife and I took a delayed honeymoon to South Africa. He reminisced about his time there as a consular officer and wished us well.

I do think Uncle Buck took secrets to the grave, but that's just my opinion.

***

On August 18, 1993, my wife took the call at our apartment on the east side of Tokyo, "Mary Lou's on the phone." I took the phone and said, "Hello." Her low voice on the other end intoned, "Buck died." Before I could offer any condolence, my aunt broke down. Losing control of her voice – the sound of which I will never forget – her words came out loudly, "Pray for his soul!"

Although Aunt Mary Lou and Buck were quiet close and she loved him dearly as a brother, she could not countenance his lifestyle. She had visited him in his years in Nassau. She had close contact with his second wife, Jerry, and later with Ingrid. She was concerned for his welfare, writing to Senator Williams, "God, through you, will help my brother."

She believed in a final judgment, the judgment referred to as the separation of the sheep and the goats in the New Testament. The sheep would inherit eternal life, and the goats would receive everlasting destruction. My uncle had expressed to Senator Williams that he would be made "the goat" of the scandal, but just in a political sense. Sadly, it appeared to my aunt that his actions and lifestyle – despite his testifying against Bobby Baker and LBJ – made him potentially face a harsh, eternal end.

Significantly, there were few people at his funeral. His sister, Genevieve, got press from the Darlington newspaper. He, on the other hand, although having had more of an impact, had been involved in scandal; even if he had come out with a whole hide, it seemed as if his hometown folk would have nothing to do with him.

He wrote no books, and the media did not write about him post scandal. It appeared that the star witness story dried up. His greatest fear, as he had also expressed to Mollenhoff, was being made the goat of the scandal. In a number of ways, that fear did come true. I do believe my uncle was, as Baker said, "no angel," and despite his testimony, he was not a hero (in a strict sense of the word) … but, in my eyes, neither was he a goat.

CHAPTER FOURTEEN

FAMILY LIFE, A RETURN TO THE SENATE, AND EXPLORING THE PAST
1993-2022

"He [Don Reynolds] and John Williams will be Profiles in Tragedy."
– Bobby Baker to Senate Historian Donald Ritchie, 2009.

My uncle left this world without any fanfare, but that didn't mean the story of Don Reynolds, Bobby Baker, and LBJ was over. On the contrary, just like smoldering embers from a fire, it still had the potential to erupt, with the slightest provocation, into a blazing flame again.

***

I spent ten years of my life in Tokyo, Japan, from 1991 to 2001, teaching English and trying to get a small business started. I married in 1992, and our only child, Emily, came along in 1998. I was completely preoccupied by the unfolding of my own life.

Aunt Ingrid travelled to Tokyo for a World Bank meeting in 1991. We met for tea at the famous Imperial Hotel, a Frank Lloyd Wright landmark. (At that time, I felt no need to go digging into details of her life with a scandalous, still living husband.) Upon her return home, Aunt Mary Lou asked her about our plans, "Are they *really* going to get married?" Marrying a Japanese national would make it, in Japanese, "kokusai kekkon," an international marriage. It seemed to be, at least for some of our family, the most important question of the year.

My dad passed in 1998. In 2001, my mom was just happy to see us come back to Madison with the new arrival of her only grandchild. Madison was a good place to live. We easily made the transition into a duplex property on Madison's east side (which we had bought in 1997), and I started working at the UW's Survey Center at Sterling Hall.

Then 9/11 happened.

***

All throughout 2001-2009, there was more news about the Baker scandal and Don Reynolds, particularly with John Simkin directing the Spartacus educational website. With the computer and knowledge revolution accelerating, practically anyone could have access to information that would have been thought inaccessible even a decade before. A simple search of "Don Reynolds" yielded a lot of information. In addition, a plethora of *New York Times* and *Time* magazine articles also popped up, as well as easy access to the LBJ secret presidential tapes that had been released ahead of schedule, in 1991.

***

When Bobby Baker returned to the Senate in 2009, he gave his legacy pitch: an interview with Senate Historian Donald Ritchie. It was Bobby's chance to set the record straight from his perspective. Of course, after all those years, misunderstandings, hyperbole, unfortunate events etc. could all be put into context, and evaluated with a critical but understanding tone. The interview was titled "Sex in the Senate." I figured that at Bobby's age, divulging information wouldn't really matter. Not to be indelicate, but people with one foot in the grave seem to be more willing to say previously unspoken truths that people with careers and other obligations wouldn't dare to utter.

What I found interesting and perplexing was that Baker used the words, "this guy Reynolds," whenever he referred to my uncle, his once longtime friend, during the interview. It seemed to create psychological distance between Baker and my uncle, and may have been used to reduce the credibility of the star witness of the '60s.

My uncle and Baker had spent a lot of time together in his Capitol Hill office. They'd had family gatherings. Uncle Buck once reminisced that I had played with the Baker kids during my summer visits (although I don't have any recollection of that).

Then, Baker referred to both my uncle and Senator Williams – in a nod to JFK's book – as "Profiles in Tragedy." Baker had survived trauma at Lewisburg Prison. He was not only a convicted felon, but had searing experiences just trying to stay alive (as vividly noted in the chapter "Surviving in the Slammer" in his book).

In Baker's view, my uncle had turned on him and did not suffer. Don Reynolds avoided prosecution – probably because he ratted on his benefactor, getting him immunity from prosecution. Just the thought of it probably burned Baker up inside. Despite his trials, I still believe that to impugn Senator Williams was a low blow. It proved to me that occasionally, time does not heal wounds, that animosities can lie just below the surface, ready to explode at any moment.

***

In his interview with Donald Ritchie, Baker mentioned a 2009 tax court decision that he wanted entered in the Senate Record. Baker indicated that the decision cleared him of the money that my uncle purportedly said he paid to Baker, but was evidently not recognized by the IRS as such. He then referred to Uncle Buck as "a lying, thieving SOB." Baker said he could never be sure enough when dealing with Reynolds.

Ritchie then added, "You had to be careful when you were dealing with people like that."

Baker was the convicted felon. My uncle was not.

I read the 2009 Senate Report, and there were a number of exchanges that disturbed me. Baker did make the admission that my uncle's testimony would have forced LBJ off the ticket in 1964. But then he changed his story on the DC Stadium and Matt McCloskey. In Baker's 1978 book, *Wheeling and Dealing*, he said my uncle told the truth about the DC stadium, adding, "I knew what the understandings were." (Bobby directing my uncle to be a go between in siphoning funds on a business transaction to a slush fund for the 1960 Johnson campaign for president.) In the 2009 interview, that version of the story disappeared. He referred to Matt McCloskey as a "nice man," then became upset, saying that my uncle made McCloskey out to be a crook.

I couldn't help but wonder if Baker had been paid to change tack.

He referred to Don Reynolds as a genius with insurance, but with strange proclivities towards sexual matters. That reflection may not have been far off the mark.

***

In 2011, my mom urged me to curtail my letter carrier duties early and get a relief carrier for the afternoon. My Aunt Jerry was coming to visit my mom at Oakwood East Retirement Village on Madison's far east side. My family request was honored, and I'm glad it was.

No sooner than I had parked the car, I heard a strong voice call, "Come on, boy!" I looked up to see my aunt standing in the doorway of the Center. She was eighty-five years old, but her voice had almost the same clarity that I remembered from when she used to call me to breakfast or lunch at her home in the early '60s. Then, as a fifty-eight-year-old man, I started running – almost as if repeating the response of my youth, not wanting to miss the great meal that she had prepared.

My mom and my aunt were quite close, but they never spoke about the past scandal. The visit was so convivial; I couldn't bring myself to disrupt it with queries about upsetting memories.

Then, in 2012, I inadvertently ran into history again. The *New Yorker* printed Robert Caro's chapter on the assassination, and my uncle's testimony. It was interesting to be working at the University of Wisconsin Survey Center, go on break, and find that *New Yorker* in the lounge room. After reading for fifteen minutes, it was back to work with health studies. (The floor where I read that magazine article was the same floor where they did army math for the Pentagon during the Vietnam War. Sterling Hall went into the history books after the massive 1970 bombing. I'd had a suspicion then that my uncle's story would also make belated headlines.)

***

Most people might agree that a half-century is a good time to stop and reflect on events. Accordingly, I attended the 2013 CAPA conference in Dallas. I know there had been speculation on LBJ's involvement in "the event."

> In December, 1966, Edward Jay Epstein wrote an article for the *Esquire Magazine* where he claimed that Reynolds had given the Warren Commission information on the death of John F. Kennedy. Reynolds said that Bobby Baker had told him that Kennedy "would never live out his term and that he would die a violent death." Baker had also said that "the FBI knew that Johnson was behind the assassination." This was later confirmed by the release of a declassified FBI file.[20]

In 2012, Phil Nelson had come out with his book *LBJ: the Mastermind of the Assassination*. It included my uncle's involvement. On page 261, he indicated that my uncle's upcoming testimony to the Senate would be the final straw that motivated LBJ to do the dirty deed.

That night, I ate dinner at a table with other conference attendees and presenters, listening to comments that the LBJ library was interested in legacy building, which meant the whole truth might not be told. I readily agreed with that summation.

20   https://spartacus-educational.com/JFKreynoldsD.htm?fbclid=IwZXh0bgNhZW0CMTA-AAR167xU9aXgWy0OeS6cntXendxmpCXBa-ScnD2OMc8mYWAcoFyNlwW52s_M_aem_ASqIDEhe-h4j6UWlfIYpegfR6jb97DSbTTnedTbj6tz0fnuHxEetEAtKV2QFDE_fPIDv4b5VMqZHnB4NCnzrbCrqk

It was hard keeping up with all of the assassination material. Doug Horne, who wrote five volumes on the assassination, asserted that the Zapruder film was doctored by the same place to which I had applied in 1984 – the National Photographic Interpretation Center. (For me, that was a strange, decades-spanning twist!)

According to Horne, a manager at the center, Dino Brugioni, maintained that there were two sets of film: the real one, and one that was sent to the Kodak facility in Rochester, NY. The Kodak version had alterations: blood spray painted on the film.

Stopping Horne in the hallway between speeches, I asked him how confident he was in his assertions. He immediately replied, "I'm 110% confident!" as he quickly strode away to another presentation.

***

One night in Madison, on the radio station the Mike 92.1, Matt Rothschild intoned, "Oliver Stone in Madison!" Stone, famous for the movie *JFK*, was coming to Mad Town. I didn't go.

***

Perhaps the most shocking and unbelievable program was aired in 2004, when the History Channel offered a rebuttal to the show "The Guilty Men." Three professors: Stanley Cutler from University of Wisconsin, Robert Dallek from UCLA, and Thomas Sugrue from Penn State – with Moderator Frank Sesno, shared their opinions on the matter.

Professor Kutler made astounding and demonstrably incorrect statements about the film describing *Guilty Men* as "deceitful, corrupt, in its entirety." When Sesno turned his line of questioning on LBJ's image to Prof. Kutler, he replied, "Sure, it's an image (to which he rolled his eyes); he's not alone in having that kind of image."

Here was a tenured professor, from a great university, ignoring evidence in a sweeping one-sentence retort. In his view, there was no connection between Bobby Baker and LBJ … but Stan Kutler was the same man who, with his intelligence and diligence, brought down Richard Nixon! It didn't seem to fit his political curriculum vitae.

Why did History Channel allow this to go unchallenged? Why wasn't Robert Caro invited to participate on the program?

Evidence was not difficult to get. It could easily be unearthed at the UW campus at the Wisconsin Historical Society, just one mile from where Professor Kutler taught his history and law classes. The LBJ presidential tapes had also been published, and of course, archives from the University of Delaware at Newark and University of Nebraska at Lincoln were available.

Kutler's almost comical response reminded me of Rodney Dangerfield's *Back to School* (actually filmed on the UW Madison campus). In the movie, Dangerfield tried to admonish the business professor about the real world – payoffs to the carpenter's union, local politicians, etc. The professor said, "That will be quite enough. It is not the kind of thing I am teaching in this class." The professor continues with his lecture and asks, "Now, where shall we site our factory?"

Dangerfield quips, "How about fantasyland?"

Was this a fantasy they were propounding on the History Channel?

Aristotle said that nature abhors a vacuum. The space left by Kutler's excuse for a rebuttal, and my uncle's advice for me to not take anybody's word inspired me – a retired postman, along with my archivist – to sift and winnow in the Wisconsin tradition, until we could fill it.

A Harvard professor added her viewpoint regarding the real world and the concepts she teaches at an elite institution, with the book *Getting to Yes*:

> As a negotiation professor, it's tricky to teach these concepts without addressing how various national & international "leaders" use these tactics. I can teach students not to use or bend to them, but they see it being used by people to maintain and acquire power. This mismatch of what I say and what they see must be addressed.

To me, it felt like her reference to "leaders" applied perfectly to LBJ. It seemed like he used every trick in the book.

Truly, it was difficult to negotiate with Lyndon and his proxy: the Senate. Actually, there really was no negotiation, only the tactics of political warfare. The worldviews of LBJ and Senator John Williams were so diametrically opposed they prevented any rational basis for bargaining.

***

In 2017, I stood before Jeff Kurz at the Madison Book Festival, playing the infamous LBJ tape about "who would destroy whom" in which LBJ talks about silencing and smearing my uncle. LBJ called my uncle "psychotic," and "a damn fool" and symbolically declared political war on him for divulging the overcharge on the RFK stadium. Kurz paused for a moment and then asked, "Was that LBJ talking about your uncle?" After I said yes, he urged me to get with the *Pathway to Publication* program.

Then, after my mother and my Aunt Ingrid passed within two weeks of each other in April 2019, the time of closure had come: I felt the need to move forward to the next chapter.

Regarding Dallas and who killed JFK … I'm agnostic, but I do believe there was motivation for LBJ to act: he would move from Vice President to President; he was naturally aggressive; he was on his home turf in Texas; and, by far the most important, his past was catching up with him – LBJ knew about my uncle's testimony slated for November 22.

I also believe that LBJ's behavior in the first year of his presidency showed the frightened reaction of a powerful man concerned about Don Reynolds.

All three men: Johnson, Baker, and my uncle, died with an asterisk besides their names – an indication that there was some complication, some unfinished business (spiritual or otherwise) … something missing from their story. It seemed as if inner demons, or some form of bitterness, attached to their souls until their very last breath.

It may seem strange that a retired postman should criticize the thirty-sixth President, but the president of United States is meant to be elected by the populace, and work for the populace. If we are willing to allow our high elected leaders to have a number of skeletons in their political closet, so be it. But I don't think it's wise to say they don't have them, or to squelch efforts to uncover them, such as was done with Lyndon Baines Johnson. The tall Texan got a free pass; he should not have.

The *Chicago Tribune* paper, November 23, 1963.

While this picture was being taken, Uncle Buck was divulging damaging information against LBJ.

CHAPTER FIFTEEN

WHAT IF?

It is my central assertion that there was not one but two intended assassinations on November 22, 1963. The first was the physical act, caused by bullets hitting the thirty-fifth president.

The second was political. Simultaneously, in New York, the press deliberated how to handle all the news.

Indeed, the affirmation of the second was buttressed by not one, but two events: *Life Magazine* was assembling a long and detailed story that would result in LBJ's demise, and my uncle, Don Reynolds, was giving information to Senate investigators in a closed, executive session that would have removed LBJ from power.

Dallas, on November 22, 1963 remains a defining historical event in our nation's history. But what would have transpired if Dallas had not happened?

The FBI's extensive surveillance of my home in Munster, Indiana would not have occurred. I might have been spared, at ten years old, the unsettling memory of two agents approaching my mom and me on that cold, snowy day. And later, I would have been spared the distress and disillusion that came from listening to secret presidential tapes that exposed LBJ's abuse of the FBI and IRS.

If Dallas had not happened, the corruption of the FBI, noted by my uncle, would not have occurred, and the huge tax judgment of the Internal Revenue Service against him probably would not have been executed. He would not have been forced to live in exile in Nassau for four years.... Perhaps my Aunt Jerry and Uncle Buck would have remained married (and I would have been able to enjoy all summers with them fulfilling their role as my godparents).

If Dallas had not happened, Don B. Reynolds might have been a hero for exposing political corruption. He would have gone down as a vindicated whistleblower and given encouragement to others to come forward in the face of venality and maladministration.

If Dallas had not happened, LBJ would have remained a relatively powerless Vice President with little, if any, influence over the Senate until JFK dumped him with corruption charges flying. Johnson would have been facing removal or impeachment from office.

But Dallas – the events of November 22, 1963 – changed everything.

Dallas gave LBJ a pardon and gave him power. It allowed him to transform into a "tyrannical King Belshazzar."

CHAPTER SIXTEEN

TRIUMPH, TRAGEDY, AND TYRANNY

Practically every LBJ memoir mentions, out of necessity, two aspects of his legacy: triumph of the Great Society, and the tragedy of Vietnam.

Our family's experience of the Johnson years prompts a re-consideration of his legacy: the addition of a third "T" – TYRANNY.

By definition, tyranny means cruel and oppressive government. It paints a picture of a government that abuses its citizens, using its agencies and surveillance to make sure dissent is nonexistent by punishing those who speak out in opposition. Tyranny is a word that can send shivers and raise blood pressure for many, including those who worry about out-of-control federal power.

Let us assess LBJ's legacy using a conventional perspective and return to the tyranny evaluation later.

Who was Lyndon Baines Johnson? "He was a difficult overbearing personality who struggled with inner demons that drove and tormented him. He had to be the best, outshine all the competition, and win at almost any cost," said presidential biographer, Robert Dallek. Dallek noted what he believed distinguished LBJ from other politicians: his degree of skullduggery. "When he broke campaign spending laws, stuffed ballot boxes, cut a political or business deal, it was always just a bit more, a little larger than what others were willing to do."[21] (Yet Dallek still believes that the only scandal that touched LBJ was Walter Jenkins being arrested at the YMCA!)

Johnson needed to prove his superiority every day; it became one of his greatest weaknesses. He didn't anticipate the courage of my uncle and the tenaciousness of Senator John Williams.

The famous evangelist Billy Graham observed that LBJ "had a conflict within him about religion" and mentioned his doubt about being "born again." "I think he tried to make up for it by having many of the outward forms of religion, in the sense of going to church almost fanatically, while he was president. Sometimes he'd go to church three times on a Sunday."

---

21   Dallek, Robert, *Flawed Giant: Lyndon Johnson and His Times, 1961-1973*, Oxford University Press 1998.

Graham mentioned that a few weeks before LBJ died, they were talking alone in his car for an hour, with the Secret Service nearby. "He was thinking spiritual things, because he didn't have long to live."

Was LBJ's conscience getting the better of him?

Bobby Baker, upon a visit to the LBJ ranch, noted a dying and bitter man. Baker was not allowed to sign the guest register; this was not a case of the Prodigal Son returning home. Baker observed "when you got right down to lick log, dealing with Lyndon Johnson was always a one-way street."

I believe these characterizations were prime factors in the efforts of the President to come out on top, using his influence with the Senate to make sure his political opponents were silenced.

LBJ had faced a formidable trio. John Williams, the "Conscience of the Senate" was unyielding, pesky, and persistent. Clark Mollenhoff, who had won almost every journalism award, would write his own book on the scandal. And Don Reynolds, the Star Witness, had decided to come clean.

So, at the end of the day, Bobby Baker, the named person of the scandal, took the fall, and my uncle was sent packing. But the real big fish had escaped. LBJ got his achievements in the Senate and his legacy secured (Vietnam excepted).

Senator Carl Curtis said that LBJ was the biggest cover-up artist he had ever seen. In a revealing oral history at the LBJ library, Curtis shared with Michael Gillette that "LBJ had this ability to make sure he wasn't touched. No, he didn't appear to be connected to the scandal at all." LBJ was content with his fruits.

***

While having a coffee with my friend, Dennis, and his wife on Madison's east side, I mentioned my exploration of my uncle's past with LBJ. Dennis reflected on the thirty-sixth President and uttered "ruthless."

I couldn't have said it better myself.

Some people are on the record to promote LBJ's legacy: tyranny? Far from it!

But there *were* tyrannical aspects of the man.

Bobby Baker was noted in the book *Lyndon*, by Merle Miller, as saying "there were a few minor scandals, but nothing that ever involved him. He was impeccably honest as far as I was concerned."

LBJ's counsel, Harry McPherson, asserted that "Johnson literally did not know a damned thing about the operations that Bobby got himself tied up in, and I know that to be the case."

Personally, I find that exceedingly hard to believe.

But despite his checkered past, my uncle decided to do a U-turn.

Robert David Johnson noted:

> While Watergate and the Lewinsky affair produced resignation or impeachment, Johnson got away with obstructing legislative and administrative inquiries. He lived in an era with a less suspicious press, and the media's almost unrelenting hostility to Goldwater caused journalists to overlook what seemed like minor indiscretions by the president.[22]

Indeed, all the investigative muster of John Williams and Carl Curtis was not enough to overturn the Senate judgment, and it has stood to this day.

***

Americans broke free from the tyranny of King George, yet Johnson thought nothing of taking the reins of government to punish a man who threatened him by deciding to come clean. Mollenhoff wrote, "Consider, then, a man such as Don B. Reynolds, who has admitted to a less-than-perfect past and who decides to turn over a new leaf. After his experience, who else like him will be encouraged to make a clean break with an unsavory past?"[23]

The Johnson family won't admit to this part of his legacy, but I believe it is indelibly part of his past; this, too, was Lyndon Johnson. None of the mainstream media has seen a need to revisit LBJ's legacy and expand it. The tyranny imprint of the thirty-sixth president should be examined, reassessed, and imparted; the Senate record – and our family's past – cries out that it must.

This legacy judgment steers clear of the controversy surrounding LBJ and the consequential events in Dallas. There are two roads that writers have opined regarding Johnson-- assassination and corruption. This story has concerned itself with corruption, not assassination.

But some judgment must be imparted. Without assassination, LBJ would have been driven from office; LBJ himself admitted on the LBJ secret tapes to his attorney Sheldon Cohen, that if he had been open and transparent, he would have gone to jail.

That legacy judgment of LBJ's corruption and tyranny still stands today. That is the lasting contribution that Don Reynolds, a whistleblower, has made to our nation's political history.

And significantly, this memoir asks us to consider questions raised for all citizens: the role of family secrets, whistleblowing, the power of federal agencies, and the threat to liberty in a surveillance society.

---

22   Johnson, Robert David, *All the Way with LBJ: The 1964 Presidential Election*, Cambridge University Press 2009.
23   *Despoilers of Democracy*, Clark Mollenhoff, 1967

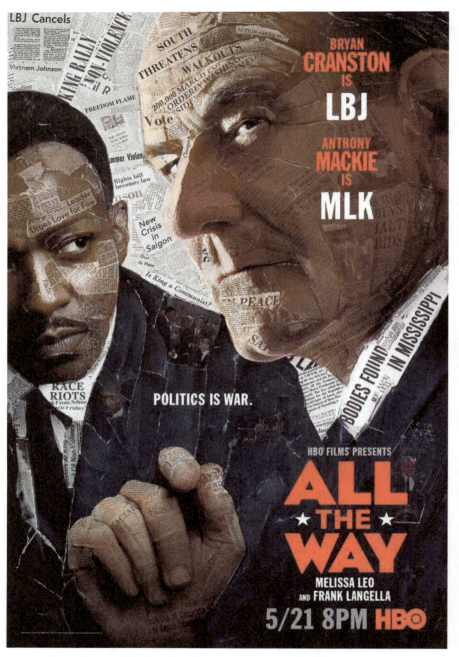

The subject is still of interest. This was a 2016 made-for-TV movie on HBO.

Postscript

"*All the Way*" was a made-for-TV movie about LBJ's first year. It covered his legislation and focused a few minutes on the problems of Walter Jenkins; nothing however, was mentioned about the conflict in testimony between Jenkins and my uncle. Clearly, there was much more to the events: the courageous man who decided to fess up, the real threats to a popular president that enveloped his political life.... Facts of history are too often lost, or glossed, in its retelling. But, as famed commentator Paul Harvey would say at the end of his broadcasts, "Now, you know the rest of the story."

This has been an account of family secrets, and more importantly, whistleblowing. The abuse of government agencies and the increasing problem of a surveillance society only adds to the conundrum.

Hopefully, more people will tell their stories and experience the twists and turns, the highs and lows, and ultimate fulfillment of exposing truth. For me, it was worth the journey, and I wish everyone the best in telling their unique pieces of the puzzle.

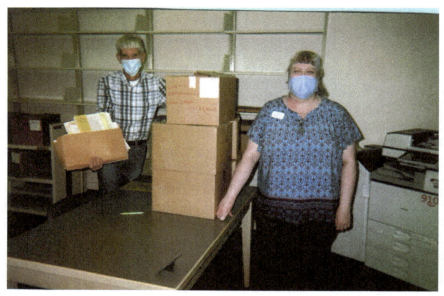

A familiar scene: digging up the archives. Research was done at universities at Wisconsin, Delaware, and Nebraska.

With archivist Matt Piersol at the University of Nebraska, Lincoln.

Epilogue

Freedom of Information Act?

By Gregory T. Smith

It has been my greatest pleasure to have been a Professional Research Historian for over thirty years. Since my academic years, I have been paid to not only research subjects of intense interest of others, but the greatest thrill is getting paid to learn new and possibly history-changing data. I have always considered myself "a kid in a candy store" in the many Archives that I have visited worldwide. Standards were instructed at the University, but I have elevated my personal standards over the years especially in examining documents from some of the greatest archival repositories in history. I was hired in October 2020 by Robert Reynolds Nelson to research government files on his Uncle, Don "Buck" Reynolds. At first, I told Robert, or "Bob" as I call him, I can't take your case. *I knew his subject would be greatly scrutinized by someone in the United States government.* In essence, I was to be hired as a Researcher and a 'Cut Out' in dealing with certain United States Government Agencies. Mainly my research was collected by petitioning the Federal Bureau of Investigation for the release of information concerning DON BUCK REYNOLDS. As I stated to Bob, this was not my first rodeo dealing with sensitive document classifications or request for (FOIPA) or Freedom of Information/Privacy Acts information from the FBI. I told Bob that I had several government inquiries before beginning many years ago. *But this inquiry for research was the first for me having to do with a former United States President and his activities just prior to then President John F. Kennedy's assassination.* This would be my second presidential request for records from the FBI. The first was some years ago dealing with the infamous General Smedley Butler supposed Plot-Coup in the 1930s. During the Smedley Butler FBI (FOIPA) request from start to finish this process was less than four months and with few redactions or roadblocks.

What I uncovered through three, painstakingly separate *Freedom of Information and Privacy Acts (FOIPA) search requests with the FBI in the Don*

"Buck" Reynolds case was staggering. I compiled this information over three years for Robert "Bob" Reynolds Nelson. However, the FBI had changed its (FOIPA) protocol. It is sad to report that the process has not been streamlined, but that task today is much more Sisyphean. This was not the shock until I began receiving correspondence back from the FBI's Record/Information and Dissemination Section of the Information Management Division. Yes, it sounds like a long title and what I experienced was even longer wait times to get information. *The entire process for Bob Nelson in regards to obtaining information from the FBI took nearly three years and sadly little from the FBI was released to date.*

This is the exact text sent from the FBI and received on July 7, 2021:

> Subject: REYNOLDS, DON BUCK
> Dear *********
>
> We're contacting you about the FOIPA request above. The FBI located approximately 17571 pages potentially responsive to your request. By letter dated March 4, 2021, you agreed to pay $535 for processing.
>
> Requests are processed in the order in which they are received through our multi-track processing system:
>
> Small track requests (0-50 pages) current average time is approximately 5 months to complete;
>
> Medium track requests (51-950 pages) current average time is approximately 31 months to complete;
>
> Large track requests (951-8000 pages) current average time is approximately 66 months to complete; and
>
> Extra-large track requests (over 8000 pages) current average time is approximately 79 months to complete.
>
> The current average time to complete your extra-large track request is at least 79 months. Reducing the scope of your request may accelerate the processing, allow for a timelier receipt of the information you seek, and reduce the duplication costs, if applicable. Would you be willing to consider reducing the scope of your request to place it in a smaller, potentially faster processing track?
>
> Please let us know if you would like to move forward with reducing the scope of your request. If you do reduce the scope of your request, you are welcome to request additional material once the last release from this request has been made.
>
> Best regards,
> FBI FOIA Negotiation Team

Epilogue – Freedom of Information Act?

What materialized in July of 2021 was that the FBI (FOIPA) process that I have performed for clients for years had a ring of now of stovepiping or Delay City. It is my opinion that this was the "shock and awe" notice. Telling me that the FBI has located 17,571 pages of "potentially" responsive material. Then the next step is that you are contacted via al U.S. Postal Service letter by Mr. Michael G. Seidel, Section Chief, Record Dissemination Section, Information Management Division, Federal Bureau of Investigation, U.S. Department of Justice. Mr. Seidel in a form letter dated February 5, 2021 informing me, "We have reviewed your request and determined it is not consistent with FBI eFOIPA [electronic receipt of Freedom of Information/Privacy Act] terms of service." As I digested this letter, and got ready to appeal, another USPS sent letter dated, February 8, 2021 arrived. This newest letter, again from Mr. Seidel or someone on his "Team," references the date of January 29, 2021 exhibiting my willingness to pay $40.00 in FOIA processing fees. That fact was indeed true. Mr. Seidel's letter to me of February 8, 2021 also exhibits my willingness to now pay $535.00 for 36 CDs at roughly $15 per CD. Releases are made on CD now unless one chooses that release to be done on paper. Then the paper release would cost $873.55 and would cover the 17,571 paper pages. Needing the entire 17,571 pages to determine if indeed these pages were correctly and "potentially" responsive to the Subject of DON BUCK REYNOLDS, one would have to personally inspect those pages. I then replied to the FBI's short form for "Requester Response" where I chose the simple sentence, "I am willing to pay estimated duplication/international shipping fees up to the amount specified in this letter." I also initialed that choice. It was assumed that this project would take months to complete. In essence 79 months. Best to allow the FBI to do their best. I had no contact with the FBI for months. We were waiting to hear from the FBI, then by coincidence we were contacted by the "Negotiation Team" of the FBI. Here is the email I received on July 7, 2021:

> FBI.FOIPA.NEGOTIATION@FBI.GOV
> Wed 7/7/2021 8:46 AM
>
> Good morning Mr. *****,
> We're contacting you about the FOIPA request above. The FBI located approximately 17571 pages potentially responsive to your request. By letter dated March 4, 2021, you agreed to pay $535 for processing.
>
> Requests are processed in the order in which they are received through our multi-track processing system:
> Small track requests (0-50 pages) current average time is

approximately 5 months to complete;

Medium track requests (51-950 pages) current average time is approximately 31 months to complete;

Large track requests (951-8000 pages) current average time is approximately 66 months to complete; and

Extra-large track requests (over 8000 pages) current average time is approximately 79 months to complete.

The current average time to complete your extra-large track request is at least 79 months. Reducing the scope of your request may accelerate the processing, allow for a timelier receipt of the information you seek, and reduce the duplication costs, if applicable. Would you be willing to consider reducing the scope of your request to place it in a smaller, potentially faster processing track?

Please let us know if you would like to move forward with reducing the scope of your request. If you do reduce the scope of your request, you are welcome to request additional material once the last release from this request has been made.

Best regards,
FBI FOIA Negotiation Team
Information Management Division

Over the next months, I heard nothing from the FBI. I assumed my FOIPA request was being fulfilled, albeit slower than my previous FOIPA requests to the FBI in previous years. Then I stumbled on some fine print with:

FOIPA Request No.: 1488434-000 Subject: REYNOLDS, DON BUCK

Dear Mr. *****:

The FBI has completed its review of records subject to the Freedom of Information/Privacy Acts (FOIPA) that are responsive to your request. The enclosed documents were reviewed under the FOIPA, Title 5, United States Code, Section 552/552a. Below you will find check boxes under the appropriate statute headings which indicate the types of exemptions asserted to protect information which is exempt from disclosure. The appropriate exemptions are noted on the enclosed pages next to redacted information. In addition, a deleted page information sheet was inserted to indicate where pages were withheld entirely and identify which exemptions were applied. The checked exemption boxes used to withhold information are further explained in the enclosed Explanation of Exemptions. Section 552 Section 552a (b)(1) (b)(7)(A) (d)(5) (b)(2) (b)(7)(B) (j)(2) (b)(3) (b)(7)(C) (k)(1) (b)(7)(D) (k)(2) (b)(7)(E) (k)(3) (b)(7)(F) (k)(4) (b)(4) (b)(8) (k)(5) (b)(5) (b)(9) (k)(6) (b)(6) (k)(7)

<u>48 pages were reviewed and 48 pages are being released</u>. Please see the paragraphs below for relevant information specific to your request as well as the enclosed FBI FOIPA Addendum for standard responses applicable to all requests. Document(s) were located which originated with, or contained information concerning, Other Government Agency (ies) [OGA]. This information has been referred to the OGA(s) for review and direct response to you. We are consulting with another agency. The FBI will correspond with you regarding this information when the consultation is completed. Please refer to the enclosed FBI FOIPA Addendum for additional standard responses applicable to your request. "Part 1" of the Addendum includes standard responses that apply to all requests. "Part 2" includes additional standard responses that apply to all requests for records about yourself or any third party individuals. "Part 3" includes general information about FBI records that you may find useful. Also enclosed is our Explanation of Exemptions. For questions regarding our determinations, visit the www.fbi.gov/foia website under "Contact Us." The FOIPA Request Number listed above has been assigned to your request. Please use this number in all correspondence concerning your request. If you are not satisfied with the Federal Bureau of Investigation's determination in response to this request, you may administratively appeal by writing to the Director, Office of Information Policy (OIP), United States Department of Justice, 441 G Street, NW, 6th Floor, Washington, D.C. 20530, or you may submit an appeal through OIP's FOIA STAR portal by creating an account following the instructions on OIP's website: https://www.justice.gov/oip/submit-and-track-request-or-appeal. Your appeal must be postmarked or electronically transmitted within ninety (90) days of the date of my response to your request. If you submit your appeal by mail, both the letter and the envelope should be clearly marked "Freedom of Information Act Appeal." Please cite the FOIPA Request Number assigned to your request so it may be easily identified. You may seek dispute resolution services by contacting the Office of Government Information Services (OGIS). The contact information for OGIS is as follows: Office of Government Information Services, National Archives and Records Administration, 8601 Adelphi Road-OGIS,

College Park, Maryland 20740-6001, e-mail at ogis@nara.gov; telephone at 202-741-5770; toll free at 1-877-684-6448; or facsimile at 202-741-5769. Alternatively, you may contact the FBI's FOIA Public Liaison by emailing foipaquestions@fbi.gov. If you submit your dispute resolution correspondence by email, the subject heading should clearly state "Dispute Resolution Services." Please also cite the FOIPA Request Number assigned to your request so it may be easily identified. See additional information which follows. Sincerely, Michael G. Seidel Section Chief Record/Information Dissemination Section Information Management Division Enclosure(s) Based on the information you provided, we conducted a main entity record search of the Central Records System (CRS) per our standard search policy. For more information about records searches and the standard search policy, see the enclosed FBI FOIPA Addendum General Information Section. This is the final release of information responsive to your negotiated FOIPA request. This material is being provided to you at no charge. A record that may be responsive to your Freedom of Information/Privacy Acts (FOIPA) request has been transferred to the National Archives and Records Administration (NARA). If you wish to review these records, submit a Freedom of Information Act (FOIA) request to NARA, Special Access and FOIA, 8601 Adelphi Road, Room 5500, College Park, MD 20740-6001. Please reference file numbers 63-HQ-8946 and 63-HQ-9953.

It has been my personal experience during the research for Bob Nelson's book, LBJ'S MORTAL WOUND: THE DON REYNOLDS STORY, that this was the most difficult, labor-intensive project that I have ever worked on. Over two years of attempting to obtain 17,000 plus pages of material taking over 79 months, searching in the main name of DON BUCK REYNOLDS. In order to get anything, I had to keep readjusting my FOIPA search to lessen my request or as the FBI calls it, "negotiation." At point for any researcher when dealing with any United States Government entity is material over time and when the negotiation ends and the material is produced. I have been a Historical Researcher for over 35 years. This project was so full of delays, roadblocks, tabling, reestablishing goalposts, and then finally when the material was being produced, it was heavily redacted. Therefore, the material was nearly worthless. However, the process soon became the focal point of my participation in Bob Nelson's fine book.

The reader will notice that the FBI states that additional information may be available at the National Archives and Record Administration

(NARA) in College Park, Maryland. I must state that I also had some disturbing experiences in my past visits to NARA at College Park, Maryland. In 2012 I was researching some old OSS files. The OSS, the Office of Strategic Services was the precursor for the Central Intelligence Agency, the CIA. I was doing this for an author who was writing a spy book about her former Nazi/British Intelligence double agent grandmother. I found great and never used before material for this author's book at NARA at College Park, Maryland. There was material in those boxes that was clearly marked, "CONFIDENTIAL," "SECRET" or "TOP SECRET." NARA has a procedure for this when one finds such materials within certain collections. In order to have those type of files within those boxes duplicated, one only needs to walk forty feet from one's personal work area desk to the Help Desk with any documents marked "SECRET" or "TOP SECRET". Then one simply hands those documents to the Textual Records Clerk who staffs this desk. This is the same desk where one has staff members pull out pins, older paper clips, metal fasteners from paper material so you can duplicate. The clerk then presents you with a duplication number waiver the size of a price tag on food products for said sensitive documents which contains the date, a tracking number, and the researcher's name. I found this procedure interesting, and I was surprised by the simplicity of the NARA procedure. After doing this procedure over days, one day I returned to NARA in the morning to find all my boxes on my cart as normal, but when I went to a particular OSS folder in one of the boxes, some of the contents of the box were missing. In their place I found a manila thick like paper folder with a small sentence on the front of the paper. It read, "Removed in accordance with the National Security Act of 1947." The rest of the manila folder was entirely clear of any other words, dates, names, or even a single letter of the alphabet. This folder was quite new. I went to NARA staff and they told me that every security Agency in the US government had offices or personnel who visit at NARA and they watch the researchers from above the Textual Records Reading Room. Although NARA's procedures are very conservative, I understand why. It's national security.

Since the FBI doesn't allow this type of research to be performed by a Professional Research Historian in person at FBI facilities, the FBI has complete and absolute control over the duplication of files and how and to whom those files are released that still reside within its Record Management Division.

The lesson for someone like me was that the FBI FOIPA procedure is in need of at least hundreds more workers to fill the backlogs of 'unassigned' requests. My request for Bob Nelson laid in 'unassigned' limbo for months before we negotiated a lower records request, so we didn't have to wait 79 months. *All we got, at no charge, were just over 40 documents heavily redacted.*

All in all, I made three separate FOIPA record requests and all FOIPA were made only to the FBI for Bob Nelson's book. Only two were only slightly successful in getting anything of use and much was redacted. One FOIPA request was a complete waste of time as there was no way we could wait 79 months for any information. Behind the wall of regulations, policies, and stovepipe procedures, I was left shaking my head over the Sisyphean task each and every time I made FOIPA request inquiries or needed to "negotiate" with FBI Dissemination Section of the Information Management Division. I don't think I would do this again as this task from the start in 2021 to this book being published in 2024 was just too much FBI policy and procedure to handle.

Photographs and Documents

I knew my Uncle Buck my whole life. We got together as family. In the bottom photo I am researching this book.

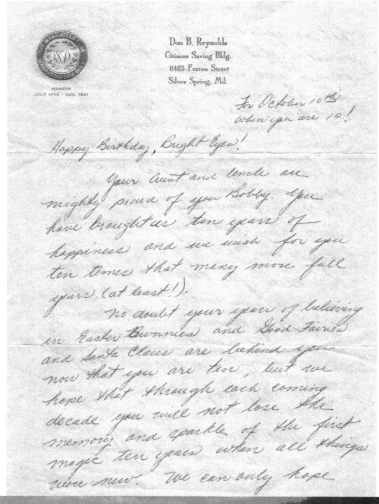

In Washington, DC as a kid, and a two-page letter to me from my Uncle Buck.

that as you learn from life — and
school — that many things are the
same — you will find something
new in each new day — in each
new task — that will have magic
in it to make you happy — and
wise.

We love your letters and we
think about you every day. We'll
be thinking especially about you on
your day — Thursday. Hope it's
a good one all day!

Bless you, darling boy. Wish
we could be with you to share
a birthday dinner — but maybe
soon — we'll manage a visit —

Know that we love you very
much, big boy. All of us —

Uncle Buck. Aunt Jerry
and Penny (who is fine, now)
and Rene (who is as bouncy
as ever.)

Bathing and swimming at Deep Creek Lake, Oakland, Maryland

Uncle Buck at one of his "power" lunches.

Don Reynolds and his girlfriends in Germany.

Uncle Buck sent me pictures of his girlfriends, and sent me a photo of a German fraulein on the right in 1969 when I was sixteen. She was the daughter of a woman he was dating.

My aunt Genevieve was the Society Writer for the Washington Post. Here, she is standing to the left of President Truman.

Senator John Williams was a four term senator from Delaware from 1947 to 1970 and "The Conscience of the Senate."

The US Department of State appoints Don Reynolds as Consul of the United States at Vienna, Austria in October 1948.

President Harry Truman appoints Don Reynolds, Foreign Service Staff Officer, as Consul of the US in 1950.

One of the payments made to my uncle – an overpayment on the DC statdium.

The National Association of Life Underwriters recognizes Don Reynolds' superior performance in life insurance underwriting in 1958. Reynolds received numerous awards for insurance underwriting. It was one reason why he was considered for underwriting LBJ's life insurance

Family was very important to my Uncle Buck, no matter his troubles, he always found time to get together. L-R, Me, Connie, (my mom), Genevieve, Reginald, May Lou and Don (Uncle Buck).

The marriage of Don Reynolds and Geraldine Witkerson. It was she who wrote, " I hope Bobby will understand someday.

things. They think that we just came out and reopened it up and built it up and got all the Congressmen and Senators all slushing away, just because we met over there at lunch the other day and decided we had to have a statement.

FORTAS: Well, Humphrey and Mansfield—

LBJ: Humphrey didn't. Humphrey told me the opposite, and Mansfield is not astute anyway. Carl Albert told me not to do it. Everybody whose judgment I really respect. And I knew it. I just knew it was bad. I just *knew* it—*instinctively*. I think it is building up now to where I think we're building it up again and I just don't like to go against your judgment 'cause you've got to defend me. If I don't follow your advice, I'm going to be in a hell of a shape. But if I *do* follow it, I'm going to *jail!* And that's the way I look at it. My instinct tells me that we're just *begging* for trouble. Just out there opening my arms by issuing these damned statements. I thought the one the other day—I just started to turn around when I started to walk out of there and I just couldn't do it because you and Clark Clifford thought it ought to be done. But I just sure think it was a terrible mistake.

---

ut 6:00 tonight I received a call from Don Reynolds. He said he s in Arizona incognito and he admitted that he was considering 1g to a country for an asylum. He said he was not in fear of his e and his wife was on the verge of a complete breakdown. The Justice Department and the Treasury Department had harrassed them to the point of destruction. He had been advised that Baker as the result of the elections had said that he was in the clear now and that they were going to get Reynolds, discredit him, and put him behind the bars, and that they would get John Williams.

They were determined to clear the case up once and for all and Baker was boastful of the fact that he was in the driver's seat even to the extent of saying that within 6 months he would be working out of the White House.

I had been undecided earlier after hearing of Mr. Reynolds' disappearance as to whether xxxxxtxkxxxxtxkxxxxxx he had been scared off or bought off. After is talking to him on the telephone I was inclided to think he was scared. His home had been burned a few months ago under rather strange circumstances, and the Departments were having someone contact all of his clients and insurance companies and they too were being harrassed to the point where they were going to be forced from doing any business with him. The

The boycott appeared to be on and they were accompanying this with the insurance company's being subpoenying records between the company, xx Mr. Renynolds, and his clients. While the companies were not involved this is an always embarrassing and could lead to the complete isolation of Mr. Reynolds and his losing all of his business connections.

In commenting on Reynolds, Bittman said that as a former government official he was ashamed of the deliberate attempt which the F. B. I., under the instructions of the Department of Justice, went out of its way to smear and discredit Reynolds as a prospective witness against Baker. The manner in which the questions by the F. B. I. were asked of the variouspeople interrogated could produce nothing but charges of Reynolds' being a liar, etc. For example, In Reynolds' testimony about the wild parties is which certain inft individuals attended their own investigation was not was such a party held and did the mentioned people attend, but ix rather, they went to these individuals and asked them if on a certain night they had an illicit affair with some woman. Automatically the xxxxanswers were no. Therefore the assumption was drawn that Reynolds was a liar. In Mr. Reynolds' statement he had not even charged that these men had slept with the women but merely that it was a wild party attended by etc., etc., etc.

A key witness in the Bobby Baker investigations, Don B. Reynolds (right), conferred with his attorney, James Fitzgerald. Reynolds was testifying before the Senate Rules Committee in the probe of Baker's affairs. AP wirephoto.

Letter from Walter Blair to Clark Mollenhoff about my uncle's troubles in Nassau.

Senator John Williams was known as "The Conscience of the Senate," and shielded Don Reynolds

I reached out to Bill Moyers about this book, I was told the Mr. Moyers "had no time."

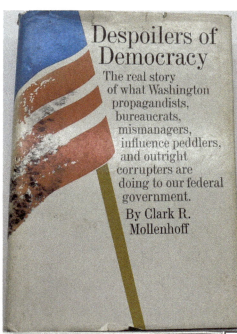
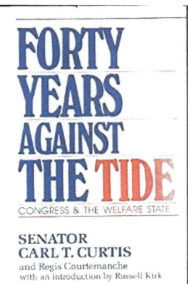
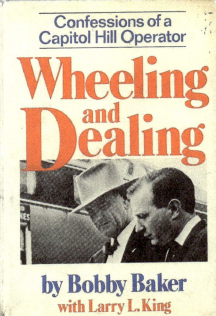
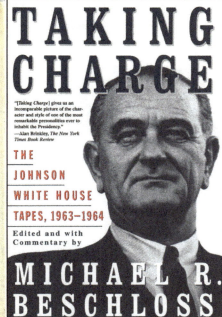

These four books have information about my uncle. Mollenhoff wrote a chapter on Don Reynolds, "Testimony During Disaster." Nebraska Senator Curtis recounts in his book the treachery in the Senate hearings. Bobby Baker in his book said my uncle told the truth about the D.C. stadium. In *Taking Charge* tells that on the tapes from January 27, 1964, LBJ said, "I am going to jail."

Index

A

Aguirre, Paul 27
All the Way with LBJ: the 1964 Presidential Election 23, 55, 121

B

Baker, Robert (Bobby) Gene 5,-8, 11, 13, 14, 19, 21, 22, 26, 27, 29-31, 34-40, 47, 48, 51, 53-55, 57, 58, 62-64, 67-71, 74, 75, 77, 80, 82, 83, 86, 88, 90, 93-97, 99, 103, 106-108, 110, 111, 118
Bauer, Joe 36
Beckman, Dan 7, 9, 52, 53, 93
Berger, Robert Winter 36
Beschloss, Michael 14, 36
Bittman, Bill 88, 89
Blair, Walter 81, 82, 91-93
Bobby Baker Affair: How to Make Millions in Washington, The 97
Bolden, Abraham 3
Bonhoeffer: Agent of Grace 67
Bonhoeffer, Dietrich 67
Boone, Richard 52
Bourne, Peter 102
Bowles, Chester 98
Brennan, Phil 21, 26
Buckley, Mike 95
Byrd, Robert viii, 6, 10, 35, 45

C

Caro, Robert 6, 8-11, 14, 28, 29, 35, 71, 110, 112
Carter, Jimmy 102
Carvel, Edwin 55
CBS Evening News 61
Central Intelligence Agnecy (CIA) viii, 8, 9, 98
Chicago Tribune 26, 31, 61
Cohen, Sheldon 8, 86, 90, 92
Connally, John 23, 98
Connally, Nellie 23
Connelly, Donald R. 57
Cooper, John 69
Cronkite, Walter 13, 39
Cumberland Gazette 9
Cumberland Times 58
Curtis, Carl viii, 7, 45, 47, 50, 54, 59, 62, 66-69, 71, 74, 118, 119

D

Dallek, Robert 8, 71, 111, 117
Dangerfield, Rodney 112
Dark Side of Lyndon Baines Johnson, The 3
Dean, John 102
Deathe, Earl 21
Despoilers of Democracy 16, 23, 27, 42, 85
Drennan, Lorin 15, 16

E

Echo from Dealey Plaza, The 3
Eklund, Roy G. 81

F

FBI viii, 2, 9, 13, 28, 33, 34, 35, 37, 38, 42, 61, 64, 65, 67, 77, 86, 88, 89, 110, 115
Ford, Gerald 96
Fortas, Abe 28, 36
40 Years Against the Tide 69
Fridge, Benjamin 37

G

Garrett County Republican 47, 52
Gatlin, Glen 23
Giancana, Antoinette 3
Gillette, Michael 118
Goldwater, Barry 58, 119
Good American Family: The Red Scare and My Father, A 6
Good Morning America 10
Graham, Billy 117, 118

H

Haley, J. Evetts 3
Harding, Warren 5, 61

Have Gun, Will Travel 52
Herald Tribune 21
Hill, Jean 1, 2
Hill, Ralph 21, 26
Hoffa, Jimmy 22, 98, 99
Hofstetter, Carol 9
Honest John Williams 9
Hoover, J. Edgar 35
Horne, Doug 111
Humphrey, Hubert 45, 93
Hutchinson, Rivinus & Co. 69

I

Internal Revenue Service (IRS) 5, 8, 9, 13, 44, 55, 57, 64, 90, 92, 104, 109, 115
It didn't start with Watergate 14

J

Jenkins, Walter 13, 21, 34-38, 45-48, 57, 58, 64, 85, 117, 121
JFK assassination 5, 23
Joesten, Joachim 3
Johnson, KC 8
Johnson, Lady Byrd viii, 45
Johnson, Luci 6, 10
Johnson, Lynda Byrd 6
Johnson, Lyndon B. (LBJ) viii, 2, 3, 5, 6, 8, 10, 11, 13, 14, 16, 21, 22, 24, 26, 28-30, 32-37, 41, 42, 45-48, 51, 55-59, 61, 68, 70-75, 79, 81, 86, 88, 90, 93-96, 98-100, 106-113, 115-119, 121
Johnson, Rebecca viii, 6
Johnson, Robert David 55, 119
Jordan, Everett 35, 43, 45, 48

K

Kai-shek, Chiang 24, 25
Katzenbach, Nicholas 61, 68
Keeler, Christine 32
Kennedy, Jackie 1, 2, 23
Kennedy, John F. (JFK) 5, 8, 10, 13, 14, 16, 22, 23, 26, 29, 71, 96, 108, 110, 111, 113, 115, 123
Kennedy, Robert (Bobby/RFK) 13, 22, 27, 28, 30, 53, 54, 66, 71, 96, 113

Kennedy vs. Johnson Chasing Demons 103
Kerr, Robert 88
Khrushchev, Nikita 98
Kutler, Stanley 10, 11, 71, 111, 112

L

Lasky, Victor 14, 54
LBJ – the Bobby Baker Scandal and the 1964 Election 55
LBJ: the Mastermind of the Assassination 111
Life (magazine) 8, 22, 29, 30, 32, 33, 74, 115
Lincoln, Abraham 7, 10, 11, 112
Luttert, Ingrid 96, 97
Luttert, Irene 97

M

Maraniss, David 6, 49, 59
McCarthy, Joe 37, 38
McClellan, Barr 10
McCloskey, Matthew 8, 13, 50, 53, 54, 56, 57, 59, 62, 65-69, 71, 74, 83, 85, 109
McCormick, John 36
McKlosky, Matt 63
McLendon, Lennox Polk (Major) 27, 34, 57, 63-66
McNamara, Bob 65
Meehan, Ellis 64
Minneapolis Star Tribune 90
Mollenhoff, Clark 6, 16, 23, 27, 28, 42, 46, 58, 77, 79, 81-83, 85, 88, 90-92, 94, 106, 118, 119
Moorman, Mary Ann 1, 2
Moyers, Bill 6, 36, 37, 58, 103
Mudd, Roger 61
Murchison, Don 86

N

National Enquirer 31
National Photographic Interpretation Center 98, 111
Nelson, Bob ii, 2, 3, 124, 128-130
Nelson, Connie Reynolds 19
Nelson, Phillip 5, 111
New York Times 35, 67, 68, 81, 100, 108

Index

Nixon, Richard 11, 93, 95, 100, 102, 112

O

Olds, Walter 26
Opinion in the Capitol 74

P

Parkinson, Eric 10
Pasek, Leonard E. 39, 40
Passage of Power, The 6, 11
Pathway to Publication viii, 113
Pearson, Drew 37-39, 41
Pincus, Walter 36
Playboy 97
Profumo, John 32, 96

R

Rada, James 9, 58
Reader's Digest 80
Reedy, George 21, 34, 71
Reynolds, Don B. (Uncle Buck) viii, x, 2, 5-9, 13-16, 19, 21, 24-29, 32-35, 38, 39, 43, 44, 47, 49-51, 53, 55-59, 61-65, 67, 69, 71-75, 77-82, 84-94, 95, 97, 99, 101-109, 113, 115, 118, 119
Reynolds, Genevieve 24, 41, 78, 89, 106
Reynolds, Jerry 7, 8, 13, 25, 27, 31, 39, 41, 51, 67, 73, 74, 84-86, 91, 96, 109, 115
Reynolds, Ingrid 19, 96, 97, 101, 103, 106, 107, 113
Reynolds, Mary Lou 24, 53, 57, 91, 97, 101, 103, 104, 105, 106, 107
Reynolds, Reginald 101, 102
Reynolds, William and Ada Spears 23
Ritchie, Donald 8, 107, 108, 109
Romestch, Ellen 96
Rosenbaum, Ron 29
Roth, Bill 73
Rothschild, Matt 111
RPI (radio program) 68
Russell, Richard 15, 45

S

Salinger, Pierre 103
Schlesinger, Arthur 99, 100
Schmidt, Helmut 96
Schreiber, G.R. 97
Scott, Hugh 46
Sesno, Frank 10, 111
Simkin, John 22, 108
Sink the Bismarck 72
Smith, Earl 61
Smith, Greg 8, 9, 11
Stegall, Mildred 45
Sun Dogs and Yellow Cake 81

T

Texan Looks at Lyndon, A 3
Thayer, Stuart 7, 52
The Guilty Men 10, 111

U

US News and World Report 57

V

Valenti, Jack 10, 36
Van Kirk, Burkett 11, 15-17, 28, 73, 103

W

Wagenvoord, James 8, 22, 30, 74
Washington Pay-Off, The 36
Washington Post 24, 34, 36, 37, 102
Washington Star 47
Wheeling and Dealing 6, 97, 98, 99, 103, 109
Wilkerson, Geraldine 7
Williams, John viii, 6, 7, 9, 11, 13, 21, 26, 27, 38, 39, 42, 47, 50, 51, 53-56, 59, 62, 64, 65, 68, 71-75, 77, 79, 80, 82, 83, 85-88, 92, 93, 96, 98, 106-109, 112, 117-119
Wisconsin Capital Times 15
Wootten, Phil 30

Z

Zapruder film 111
Zuckert, Eugene 37
Zweifel, Dave 15

Addendum I

A Tale Of Three Cities – What The Dickens Are Ya Talkin' 'Bout?!

A prolific author wrote many books a long time ago. *A Christmas Carol, David Copperfield, Great Expectations, Oliver Twist* and a whole bunch of others. One of his most famous books is *A Tale of Two Cities* – published in 1859. Many of his works have been made into movies. *A Tale of Two Cities* is about London and Paris and starts out famously with: "It was the best of times, it was the worst of times." I'm talking about author Charles Dickens, of course.

Well, to follow below are two short stories about "A Tale Of Three Cities":

Part One: A Tale Of Three Cities: Chicago – Miami – Dallas. November 2nd, 18th & 22nd, 1963

It seems that there were several plans in the works for the "removal" of President Kennedy. He was scheduled to come to Chicago on Saturday, November 2nd, 1963, for an Army - Air Force football game at Soldier Field. Abraham Bolden of the Chicago Secret Service office has detailed that there appeared to be a plot in the works to kill Kennedy when he came to town to watch this sporting event. The White House was notified, at the last moment, and President Kennedy canceled his trip to Chicago. This story isn't brand new, but there is a book that just came out in 2024 by famous J.F.K. assassination researcher Vince Palamara called *The Plot To Kill President Kennedy in Chicago* – published by TrineDay. If J.F.K. had been killed in Chicago twenty days before he ended up dying in Dallas on Friday, the 22nd, we'd probably never know of a guy named Lee Harvey Oswald. He might, believe it or not, even be alive today at the age of eighty-five, as I write this – having been born in October of 1939. And the clock was ticking…

President Kennedy visited Miami, Florida on Monday, November 18th, 1963 – just four days before he ended up being murdered in Dallas, Texas on Friday, the 22nd. The local police had determined, through informant Willie Somersett, that there might be an attempt on the President's life and the motorcade was called off. Joseph Milteer was secretly recorded describing an assassination attempt on President Kennedy on November 9th. The motorcade was called off. Kennedy got to live for another four days. If he had been killed in Miami, we most likely wouldn't even know who Lee Harvey Oswald was. And the clock was ticking...

November 22nd, 1963. Friday. Dallas, Texas. The clock was ticking. Kennedy is shot to death on a public street in an open limousine. His wife Jackie is sitting right next to him. She is splattered with blood and brain matter. Lee Harvey Oswald is arrested. He proclaimed his innocence: "I didn't shoot anybody, no sir ... I'm just a patsy." Two days later, on Sunday, the 24th, he is shot to death in front of dozens of police officers and journalists by a man named Jack Ruby in the Dallas Police Station, as he [Oswald] is about to be transferred from the City Jail to the County Jail. This was all on live television. He never lived to have a trial. He goes down in history as an infamous evil man.

Because Kennedy died in Dallas that Friday, we know who Oswald is. By the way, I believe that Lee Oswald never did shoot J.F.K. And the clock – as well as Kennedy's heart – stopped ticking.

PART TWO: A TALE OF THREE CITIES: DALLAS – WASHINGTON, D.C. – NEW YORK. FRIDAY, NOVEMBER 22ND, 1963

Just as President Kennedy was being shot to death in Dallas on Friday, November 22nd, 1963, Don Reynolds, the uncle of author Bob Nelson, was giving testimony under oath to the Senate Rules Committee about Vice President Lyndon Johnson in Washington, D.C. This was concerning kickbacks, financial bribery and extortion. In Phillip F. Nelson's 2010 book "L.B.J.: The Mastermind of J.F.K.'s Assassination" – he writes that Johnson "had to proceed as planned and Kennedy had to die on November 22. After that, it would be too late to contain the problem presented by the new witness, Mr. Reynolds." This is on page 269 of the hardcover version of the book. At just about the same time that these events were happening in Dallas and Washington, D.C., there were some important things going on in New York City, as well. James Wagenvoord was an associate editor at "LIFE" magazine.

They were getting ready to put out a major news piece in their next issue about Vice President Lyndon Johnson. "LIFE" had been working on it for a while. The article would have exposed corrupt activities by

Johnson, involving Billie Sol Estes and Bobby Baker. It's quite possible that L.B.J. would have been finished, taken off the 1964 ticket and maybe would have faced prison time. Kennedy would have picked someone else as his V.P. running mate. So – three important things were essentially happening at the same time in Dallas, in Washington, D.C. and in New York City: the President of the United States was being shot to death in Dallas, Don Reynolds was giving sworn testimony against Vice President Johnson in D.C. and "LIFE" magazine was getting ready in New York to put out an article that would have destroyed L.B.J.'s political career. "LIFE" quickly decided to terminate the scandalous story on Johnson and go with an article about Kennedy's assassination instead. They had purchased the rights fairly quickly to the [Abraham] Zapruder film of J.F.K.'s murder on Elm Street in Dallas and select frames from that home movie were displayed in the next issue of the magazine. "LIFE" magazine's sordid story on Lyndon Johnson, who became the President upon Kennedy's death, disappeared forever.

–Phil Singer, Illinois, February 2025.

Addendum II

Getting Closer To The Truth

New Information On President Kennedy, Lyndon Johnson And Don Reynolds, etc.

While there is nothing wrong with the "old" evidence, new information continues to come out concerning President Kennedy's assassination and Lyndon Johnson and Don Reynolds, etc. This is encouraging, because we're hopefully getting closer to the truth. That is why we shouldn't give up hope in our historical researching. To follow are just a few of many relatively recent examples of what I'm referring to.

A book came out in 2020 called "The Lone Star Speaks: Untold Texas Stories about the J.F.K. Assassination" by Katana Zachry and Sara Peterson. This book is a wonderful contribution to the J.F.K. case. There are seventy short chapters about numerous aspects of the case. It contains many, many new and important stories from a whole lot of people about Kennedy, Lyndon Johnson, Lee Oswald, Jack Ruby and others. The authors have done a diligent job of documenting their years of studying the case and their extensive interviews. There's a tremendous amount of new information in this book that you won't find anywhere else.

"Admitted Assassin: Roscoe White and the Murder of President Kennedy" is a book that came out in 2023. It was written by Ricky White, J. Gary Shaw and Brian K. Edwards. This is the story of Ricky's father Roscoe White. It makes a compelling case that Roscoe may have been the shooter of J.F.K. from behind the picket fence on the grassy knoll in Dealey Plaza. Quite possibly Roscoe was also the shooter of Dallas Policeman J.D. Tippit around forty or so minutes later. Gary Shaw, as he is called, is a long-time, very well-respected Kennedy researcher. He even knew Jack Ruby. Shaw has been studying the case pretty much since it happened and has interviewed many witnesses and people related to the topic. The book contains lots of documents and photos, helping to tell this amazing story.

Recently, a new story came out about Billie Sol Estes, who was an associate of L.B.J. It has been rumored for years and years that Estes had some tapes or recordings of, or about, Lyndon Johnson. Well, in 2009, I was at home with a friend, who had an extensive amount of information on the Kennedy case. We got to talking about Bilie Sol Estes and I said that I had his phone number. My friend [Dave] couldn't believe it. I said, "Should we give him a call?" Dave was fairly excited and said, "Yeah. Let's call him up." So I called Billie Sol. I talked with his daughter Pamela. She said that she'd have Billie Sol call us back. And sure enough, about half-an- hour later or so, my phone rang. Yep. It was Billie Sol. I said, "It's been rumored that you have these audio tapes or recordings about L.B.J. or with L.B.J." He confirmed it, but stated that: "They're doing a movie about me and they're paying me fifty-one million dollars and I can't talk about it." Well, I knew that that dollar amount couldn't be right, but maybe he was getting some significantly lower monetary figure. Dave wanted to talk with him, so I handed the phone to Dave. Within the last month or two, a story broke that Billie Sol's grandson Shane Stevens released a tape of Billie Sol talking with Cliff Carter, a key Lyndon Johnson associate. This conversation appears to have taken place in 1971, shortly before Carter died. Billie Sol Estes and Cliff Carter discuss the fact that Lyndon Johnson had a different associate [Mac Wallace] hired to assassinate President Kennedy. Carter says: "Lyndon never should have issued that order to Mac." The tape was released on the internet and appears to be legitimate. I contacted Billie Sol's grandson Shane Stevens and we talked on the phone for some thirty or forty minutes. Shane's had the tape for around nine years or so. And more tapes may exist and come out.

Abraham Bolden is a good friend of mine. He is ninety years old and lives in Chicago. He was handpicked by President Kennedy to be the first "Negro" Secret Service agent on the White House detail in the spring of 1961. For many years, he wouldn't publicly discuss an incident that he observed in the White House between L.B.J. and the Kennedy brothers, John and Robert. [Watch the video interview on the internet that I did with Mr. Bolden by going to "Abraham Bolden: L.B.J. Threatens J.F.K. 1961" - it's 5:45 long.] The argument between Johnson and the Kennedy brothers took place in the Oval Office. Mr. Bolden was in the hallway as a Secret Service agent on duty. But he heard a lot of yelling and swearing. When Johnson came out of the room, he stood there looking at the Kennedys and said something like: "You sons-of-bitches better quit fuckin' with me!" Well, Abraham took it as a serious threat to the President and reported it to his superiors. When I asked him what Johnson and the Kennedy brothers were arguing about in the Oval Office that day, he basically said that he didn't know or couldn't make it out. But not all that long ago, he told me that he recalls hearing the name of Billie Sol Estes and stuff about cotton. Billie Sol was involved in a big cotton allotment incident and ended up in real trouble due to it. Abraham chose not to include this story about L.B.J and President Kennedy and his brother Robert in his own book "The Echo From Dealey Plaza" that came out in 2008. But now it's out there.

In 2021 a book came out called "Lucky Conversations" by Morris Wolff. Mr. Wolff met President Kennedy in April of 1963, about a half-a-year before Kennedy was killed in Dallas. For a while, he would personally hand-deliver documents and messages between the Kennedy brothers in Washington, D.C. as they were concerned that their phones were tapped by the Director of the F.B.I. - J. Edgar Hoover. Amazing, huh? After J.F.K.'s death in late-November of '63, Wolff became the chief legislative assistant to Senator John Sherman Cooper, who was one of the members of the Warren Commission. He would drive Cooper to and from the Warren Commission hearings and meetings. And they would talk about the evidence in the J.F.K. case. Here are just a few statements that Wolff quotes Warren Commission member Cooper as saying: "Jack Kennedy was a goner as soon as he stepped off the plane in Dallas …. Oswald was a fall guy … Kennedy was a dead duck … it was a setup. There was no real security provided in Dallas. Security stepped aside and let the tragedy happen." Cooper told Wolff that Johnson was involved in Kennedy's death. And that there had to have been at least two gunmen involved. Wolff kept this story to himself for decades. But it's all detailed now in his book.

Bob Nelson, the author of the book that you're holding, also has some new information. He has an acquaintance that prefers not to be named. Bob has gone over this story many, many times with this person. The story goes like this: J. Edgar Hoover - the head of the F.B.I. - contacted Bob's uncle Don Reynolds in 1964. Hoover said to Reynolds: "Don, you and I are both Masons. In that spirit, I want to tell you this. Leave the States. Don, leave the States. If you don't, L.B.J. will kill you." Whoa! Don Reynolds, the uncle of this book's author Bob Nelson, did leave the United States for four to five years until L.B.J. was out of office. He only came back for Congressional testimony while Johnson was the President.

So - new information does continue to come out, adding to the things that we already know about the events that took place in the 1960s with President Kennedy, Lyndon Johnson, Billie Sol Estes and the Warren Commission. And Don Reynolds too. Let's hope that even more information will continue to come out so that we can get closer to the truth of what really happened back in the 1960s. Truth-seekers: hang in there. Don't give up searching for the facts.

-Phil Singer, Illinois, February 2025.

Addendum III

What's New? What's Old? The J.F.K. Files, etc. – February 2025

"If Lee Harvey Oswald assassinated President Kennedy by himself, planned the whole affair alone and received no other assistance or finance from anyone else (the [Warren] Commission's main conclusions), then why: twelve years after the assassination aren't these documents released - if that's all they will show?" That was written by a young college student in his school's newspaper on September 23, 1975. That's fifty years ago now - a full HALF-CENTURY ago. Well, the person who wrote that was me. I was twenty at the time and going to Knox College in Galesburg, Illinois. I was a part of the Citizens Commission of Inquiry organization, headed up by Mark Lane, who wrote "Rush To Judgment" in 1966 - one of the first and best books about the J.F.K. case. We were trying to get the case reopened. And get the classified files released to the public. I was writing letters on my typewriter at night to Senators and Congressmen, encouraging them to reopen the John F. Kennedy case and release the files - the documents that were still hidden away from the public.

I would get letters back from these Senators and Congressmen. I still have many of them. This all led to the formation of the House Select Committee on Assassinations in 1976. So - I guess that I played a small role in helping to get the case reopened. I tried to work for the H.S.C.A., but got turned down. I suspect that it was because they knew that I was a part of the C.C.I. organization. I have the letter that they wrote me. The H.S.C.A. did acknowledge that there appeared to be a shot fired from the infamous grassy knoll, but that the shot didn't hit anything. It didn't strike any of the occupants of the limousine or the vehicle itself. It missed everything. This conclusion was primarily based upon acoustical evidence: an analysis of the audio recording from the exact time of the shooting. The H.S.C.A. in 1979 - like the Warren Commission in 1964 - locked away a whole bunch of evidence for many, many years. But the House Select Committee on Assassinations did state that Kennedy "was probably assassinated as a result of a conspiracy." It seems that most people don't know - or remember - that nowadays. The H.S.C.A. asked the Department of Justice to follow-up. It appears, sadly, that the D.O.J. didn't do anything.

So - as I'm writing this in February of 2025, it's been reported recently that the J.F.K. files will finally be released soon. And maybe those too covering Martin Luther King, Jr. and Robert F. Kennedy - both of whom were shot to death in 1968. Over the years some documents have been released to the public, but many of them have been partially – or highly-redacted. That means a lot of information has been blacked out – things like names, dates, places and events. Over the years, I have learned that some of the documents are not authentic. Some people have personally told me that. One example is Don Adams. He was an F.B.I. agent back in 1963. When he saw some of the reports that he wrote many years later - reports that he person- ally wrote in '63 related to the J.F.K. case - some things were changed. He basically said to himself, "That's not what I wrote. This was changed around." Adams was quite understandably upset that some of his reports had been altered and he documented his story in a book – "From an Office Building with a High-Powered Rifle" in 2012 and published by TrineDay. I helped him with some of the research that went into the book. Jean Hill was a witness to the J.F.K. killing. I knew her too. She stated that some of her testimony was changed. Another witness, S.M. Holland, said the same thing. Holland claimed that at least one shot was fired from behind the picket fence and he saw a puff of smoke linger in the air in that same area. He also claimed that he heard at least four shots fired. A Deputy Sheriff, Roger Craig, claimed that the rifle found in the Texas School Book Depository was a German Mauser, as did others. And he stated that Oswald left the Dealey Plaza area by getting into a station wagon driven by someone else. He was discredited. The Warren Commission said that the rifle was an Italian Mannlicher- Carcano. And that Lee Oswald left the scene of the crime by a bus and a cab. Julia Ann Mercer, saw some suspicious things on Elm Street before the assassination of President John Kennedy. She saw a person that she thought was Jack Ruby in a pick-up truck, where a young man got out and appeared to carry what looked like a rifle case up the grassy knoll. Mercer said that the signature on her affidavit was not hers and that some of the details on it were false. Etc. Etc. Etc. Evidence is only meaningful if it's for real – if it's genuine. And is not obscured by a whole lot of black ink that obscures the contents of the documents.

I am writing about this because maybe - just maybe - some of the documents that might be released soon, or whenever, might be documents that mention Don Reynolds. Or the author of this book, Bob Nelson. There could be F.B.I. – or other government - reports that discuss the testimony of Reynolds. Maybe there will be reports about the whereabouts of Reynolds when he fled the country due to threats upon his life. Author Nelson had his house surveilled by the F.B.I. in Munster, Indiana in the mid-'60s when he was just a young boy. Are there reports about this that still exist? Perhaps. So - let's hope that the truth – the full truth – comes out about Don Reynolds and his nephew Bob Nelson. And that the documents are authentic and haven't been changed around. Additionally, let's hope that the pages are not all blacked-out by a Magic Marker or Sharpie-type of pen, leaving the information virtually meaningless.

–Phil Singer, Illinois, February 2025.